THE
Everyday Vegan
CHEAT SHEET

Skyhorse Publishing books may be purchased in bulk at special discounts for sales promotion, corporate gifts, fund-raising, or educational purposes. Special editions can also be created to specifications. For details, contact the Special Sales Department, Skyhorse Publishing, 307 West 36th Street, 11th Floor, New York, NY 10018 or info@skyhorsepublishing.com.

Skyhorse® and Skyhorse Publishing® are registered trademarks of Skyhorse Publishing, Inc.®, a Delaware corporation.

Visit our website at www.skyhorsepublishing.com.

10 9 8 7 6 5 4 3 2 1

Library of Congress Cataloging-in-Publication Data is available on file.

Cover design by David Ter-Avanesyan
Cover photo by Hannah Kaminsky
Edited by Leah Zarra

Print ISBN: 978-1-5107-6865-9
Ebook ISBN: 978-1-5107-6866-6

Printed in China

THE *Everyday Vegan* CHEAT SHEET

A Plant-Based Guide to **One-Pan** Wonders

HANNAH KAMINSKY

Skyhorse Publishing

Contents

INTRODUCTION   VII
No Sheet, Sherlock   vii
Recipe for Success   viii
Ingredient Glossary   x

BREAKFAST   1
Apple-Cinnamon Peanut Butter Bostock   3
Banana Sheet Pan Cakes   4
Black Bean Chilaquiles   7
Cinnamon Sugar Sweet PotaToast   8
Confetti Cake Granola   11
Denver Omelet Roulade   12
Frosted Corn Flakes   15
Oatmeal Cookie Baked Oatmeal   16
Spiralized Hash Browns   19
Sunrise Scramble Sandwich   20
Super-Sized Pop Art Tart   23
Tofu Shakshuka   26

SNACKS & APPS   29
Cauliflower Tempura   31
Dill Pickle Chickpea Crunchies   32
Falafel Panisse with Whipped Tahini   35
Furikake Avocado Fries   38
Greens and Beans Crostini   41
Hot Smashed Hummus   42
Mushroom Larb   45
Nacho Mamma Loaded Tortilla Chips   46
Oatsome Energy Bars   49
Okonomiyaki   50
Pretzel Focaccia   53
Puppy Training Treats   54
Sour Cream and Onion Zucchini Chips   57
Super Corny Quesadilla   58

SALADS   61
All-Kale Caesar   63
Aloha Ramen Slaw   64
Blistered Green Bean Niçoise Salad   67
Charred Broccoli Crunch Salad   68
Crispy Kale Salad   71
Curried Naan Panzanella   72
Greek Three-Bean Salad   75
Perfect Picnic Potato Salad   76
Pesto Tabbouleh   79

Southwestern Wedge Salad   80
Tofu Caprese   83
Warm Brussels Sprouts Salad   84

SIDES   87
Baby Corn Esquites   89
Broiled Bhindi Masala   90
Corn Pudding   93
Jalapeño Cornbread   94
Melting Za'atar Potatoes   97
Miso-Ginger Glazed Carrots   98
Nuthouse Stuffing   100
Pumpkin Parker House Rolls   102
Sauerkraut Colcannon   104
Scalloped Summer Squash   107
Snappy Snap Pea Risotto   108
Spicy Sichuan Snow Peas   111
Steakhouse Cabbage with Horseradish Cream   112

SOUPS & STEWS   115
Canh Chua   117
Championship Four-Pepper Chili   118
Chipotle Pozole   121
French Onion Soup   122
Garlicky Greens and Beans Stew   125
Minestrone Primavera   126
Mushroom Barley Soup   129
Pumpkin Khichdi   130
Roasted Tomato Gazpacho   133
Roasted Zucchini and Chickpeas en Brodo   134
Ruby Beet Borscht   137
Yaki Udon Noodle Soup   138

ENTREES   141
BBQ Baked Bean Loaded Potatoes   143
Chakalaka   146
Chickpea Pan Pie   149
Chickpea Tikka Masala   150
Dengaku Donburi   153
Dirty Riced Cauliflower   154
Eggplant Shawarma   157
General Tso's Tofu   158
Harvest Tagine   161
Hungry, Hungry Hippie Panini   164
Jerk Seitan with Tostones   167

Kabocha Gnocchi with Miso Browned Butter   168
Lavash Lasagna   171
Low Country Broil   172
Mad Mac & Peas   175
Paella Huerta   176
Portobello Paprikash   179
Sheet Loaf with Mashed Cauliflower   180
Sheet Pan Pizza   183
Soy Curl Bulgogi with Broccoli   186
Spaghetti Squash Bolognese   189
Sweet Sesame Tofu and Roasted Brussels Sprouts   190
Tempeh Piccata   193
Tofu Fried Rice   194

DESSERT   **197**
Apricot-Almond Clafoutis   199
Brownie Crisps   200
Carrot Cake Roulade   203
Cherry-Cola Texas Sheet Cake   205
Double Dark Fudgewiches   208
Indoor S'mores   211
Jumbo Crumb Apple Crumble   214
New York Crumb Cake   217
Peaches and Cream Cobbler   218
Peanut Butterscotch Blondies   221
Strawberry-Rhubarbarian Bars   222
Thai Tea Sheet Cake   225
Whole Coconut Haupia   226

Index   228
Conversion Charts   239

Introduction

What's so special about sheet pans? I can't recall anyone waxing rhapsodic about such a ubiquitous, unremarkable slab of metal, and yet, their rise in popularity has steadily grown over the years, building slowly and steadily. Don't call it a trend because it's not a passing phase—already having withstood the test of time, sheet pans aren't going anywhere.

What makes them so special is the fact that they aren't. Everyone has one or two, or if you're like me, closer to twenty. They won't buckle under the blast of a 450-degree oven, nor the icy tundra of the freezer. Beyond baking, there's nothing like a sheet pan to help convey a full battery of ingredients, display a finished dish, or even build a table centerpiece for the truly crafty.

While many cooks would claim a knife to be the most crucial tool in the kitchen, there's a compelling argument to be made for the humble sheet pan. One-pot cookery gets all the love lately, especially with the invention of slick electronic pressure cookers and air fryers, with all their bells and whistles. Let's shift that perspective to focus in on one-pan cookery instead, for the numerous, obvious benefits.

Entire meals take shape on a single sheet, enabling you to feed a crowd with minimal effort, little cleanup, and zero stress. Forget about the initial cost barrier of a fancy new gadget; if you somehow have made it this far in life without any sort of sheet pan, I promise you're not far from one. If you're not convinced, borrow one from a neighbor, invite them over for dinner, and you'll see that it's well worth a few extra dollars.

From oven to table, prepare yourself for a veritable sheet show once you get started. Sheet, yes!

NO SHEET, SHERLOCK

Before we start cranking up the oven and busting out the knives, we need to begin with the single most critical question of all: What *is* a sheet pan, exactly? In the broadest terms, a sheet pan is a baking tray with a shallow rim around all four sides. They're most frequently made of aluminum, but are also available in stainless steel, carbon steel, copper, ceramic, and even silicone.

Nonstick options add a thin layer of polytetrafluoroethylene (PTFE), also known as Teflon™, over that base, but I don't recommend going this route. This coating makes them more prone to warping over time, scuffing, and uneven cooking, to say nothing of the potential for chemical off-gassing at high temperatures. Baking aids like parchment paper or aluminum foil come in handy here to add an extra layer of defense over sticking for any pan!

Good old aluminum is the industry standard; peek into any commercial kitchen and you'll see shelves stacked high with these weathered silver workhorses. They're cheap, readily available the world over, and found in the greatest range of sizes. Functionally, they're exceptionally heat-conductive, which means they can brown food quickly and cool down just as fast out of the oven.

Speaking of sizes, here's where most people get into trouble. The most common dimensions are 18 × 13-inches, which is referred to as a half-sheet pan. That may look big to the average home cook, but it really is only the middle child in this family. A full sheet pan is 18 × 26-inches; larger than will fit in most household ovens. Designed for big batches in restaurants and industrial cooking applications, you're unlikely to come across these behemoths in a consumer cookware store. So then, what's smaller than a half? A quarter, of course! As you might have guessed, quarter sheet pans measure 9 × 13-inches, which is also the same size as many rectangular baking dishes. This is good to know in case you're dealing with a particularly saucy or soupy recipe and want to take out a bit of extra insurance against splashes or spills.

What, then, is a jelly roll pan? Yes, these are also sheet pans, but in a whole different category of measurement. These are 10 × 15-inches, designed primarily for roll cakes, of course. Can you cook a recipe designed for a half sheet pan in a jelly roll pan? Yes! Can you bake a cake made for a jelly roll pan in a half sheet pan? No! Baking demands more precision, which includes specific pan sizes to achieve the proper thickness of batter. It just won't cook through properly otherwise, and no one wants either a dry or soggy crumb.

For teeny tiny batches, there are indeed one-eighth sheet pans, clocking in at a mere 9 × 6-inches. These are really intended for use in toaster ovens, though they can be handy if you're scaling down a recipe to cook for one.

Finally, let's not forget about cookie sheets. Either completely flat or with just one raised lip, cookie sheets are not sheet pans. There's no standard of measurement, they're typically made of thinner or lighter material, and anything with even a drop of moisture will end up splattering all over the bottom of your oven. Let's leave those in the cabinet for this round, shall we?

RECIPE FOR SUCCESS

Stomach growling, mouthwatering, the best and worst time to crack open a new cookbook is when you're already hungry. Temptation to skip ahead, skim through instructions, or make wild substitutions is at an all-time high. I get it, and I'm guilty of the same crime! For your best results, take an extra minute to make sure you get it right.

A good recipe should guide you from beginning to end easily, like a friend coaching you in the kitchen, answering questions before they even bubble up to the surface and teaching you a thing or two along the way. Eventually, you should understand the mechanics of the procedure well enough to riff on them to create your own culinary masterpiece, tailored to your unique preferences. For the first time out of the gate, though, try to stick to the instructions as written, at least if you want your meal to look like the photo. I promise, there's no trickery here; what's pictured is exactly what you'll get if you play by the rules!

Read through the entire recipe first so there are no unpleasant surprises. Things can happen quickly under high heat, so you want to be prepared for the potential of splashing or burning and be ready to prevent it from happening.

Don't miss the headnotes or text boxes! Though there's usually a bit of storytelling that describes the origin or inspiration for the dish, it's helpful for getting a better idea of what it will taste like and look like, so you'll know when you get it right. Plus, you might pick up on tasty serving suggestions for rounding out the meal, or a few fresh ideas for flavor variations that could be even more appealing than the base formula as written.

Assemble all the ingredients, prepare them as described, measure them out, and have them easily accessible. This is what the French call *mise en place*, or "everything in place." You'll be able to speed through the instructions without pausing to chop an onion midway through the cooking process or realizing at the last minute that you don't actually have that can of beans you could have sworn was in the back of the pantry.

Measure twice, cut once, as the proverb would advise. This is applicable to much more than carpentry and sewing. Take care to properly account for your ingredients. That means leveling off measuring cups for an even, complete fill, packing brown sugar firmly to make sweet little sandcastles when unmolded, or going for a higher level of accuracy by using weight measures. Flour and other similarly powdery ingredients are one of the most frequently mismeasured substances, simply because the method can affect the results drastically. Always sift flour into the measuring cup, overfill, and then sweep the excess back into the bag with the back of a knife for a flush fill. If you scoop it straight out, you'll compact the ground grains which could almost double the total amount. I'm a huge fan of using a kitchen scale to cut out variables and also reduce the number of implements to wash at the end of the day. Check out page 239 for some quick volume to weight conversions.

Ingredient wording matters, too! The way that various foods are accounted for in the ingredient list, including punctuation and order, is carefully considered from the beginning of recipe development. "2 cups strawberries, sliced" means something very different from "2 cups sliced strawberries." The former means to measure whole berries, and then slice them. The latter, however, means that you should first slice the berries and then measure the slices.

Pay attention to ingredient specifications. Bread flour is not the same as all-purpose flour nor cake flour; each subtle variation is employed for a reason. While the recipe may technically work with a substitution, it won't necessarily be as good. This is especially true for salt. Unless otherwise specified, the "salt" that I call for in recipes is just plain table salt. Pickling salt is incredibly fine, which means you're packing a much saltier punch for every teaspoon. On the other end of the scale, kosher salt is much larger, so your food may taste comparably unseasoned or lacking by following the same measurements.

Don't get it twisted. Sheet pans can become warped over time from rapidly heating and cooling, which can cause parts to expand and contract at different rates. This is exacerbated when the hot metal is quenched with cold water. Avoid this harsh treatment at all costs! Although you can still technically use warped sheet pans, they're more prone to leakage, splashing, or spilling when accommodating recipes with more liquid ingredients. Once bent out of shape, there's no going back. Replace aging equipment before it becomes a liability.

Make sure your oven is properly calibrated. The digital readout is rarely accurate, even in brand new models, so it's wise to keep at least one independent thermometer inside the oven. These, too, can be notoriously unreliable, so I like to use two or three thermometers hanging on different racks, so I can base my calculations on the average from those readouts.

Though it can be tough to cut down on distractions, try to make your time in the kitchen a fun activity, worthy of your full attention. You'll enjoy the process more, have better control over each step, and maybe, just maybe, carve out a little time to relax along the way.

INGREDIENT GLOSSARY

Agave Nectar

Derived from the same plant as tequila but far less potent, this syrup is made from the condensed juice found at the core of the agave cactus. It is available in both light and dark varieties; the dark possesses a more nuanced, complex, and somewhat floral flavor, while the light tends to provide only a clean sweetness. Considered a less refined form of sugar, agave nectar has a much lower glycemic index than many traditional granulated sweeteners, and is therefore consumed by some diabetics in moderation.

All-Purpose Flour

While wonderful flours can be made from all sorts of grains, beans, nuts, and seeds, the gold standard in everyday baking and cooking is still traditional "all-purpose" wheat flour. Falling texturally somewhere in between cake flour and bread flour, it works as a seamless binder, strong foundation, and neutral base. It's an essential pantry staple for me, stocked in my cupboard at all times. All-purpose flour may be labeled in stores as unbleached white flour or simply "plain flour." Gluten-free all-purpose flour is also widely available now in mainstream markets and can be substituted at a 1:1 ratio for those sensitive to wheat. Many different blends exist, but I've personally had good results with Bob's Red Mill®, Cup 4 Cup®, and King Arthur®.

Almond Meal/Flour

Almond flour is nothing more than raw almonds ground down into a fine powder, light and even in consistency which makes it ideal for baking, while almond meal is generally a bit more coarse. To make your own, just throw a pound or so of completely unadulterated almonds into your food processor, and pulse until floury. It's helpful to freeze the almonds in advance so that they don't overheat and turn into almond butter. You can also create a finer texture by passing the initial almond meal through a fine sieve to sift out the larger pieces. Due to their high oil content, ground nuts can go rancid fairly quickly. If you opt to stock up and save some for later, be sure to store the freshly ground almond flour in an airtight container in the refrigerator or freezer. To cut down on labor and save a little time, almond flour or meal can be purchased in bulk from natural food stores.

Aquafaba

It's the not-so-secret ingredient taking the world by storm, dubbed a "miracle" by some and a food science breakthrough by others. In case you're not already a fervent fan, aquafaba is the excess liquid found in any ordinary can of chickpeas. Technically, any bean can produce aquafaba, but the unique ratios of protein and starch found in garbanzo beans has been found to best mimic the unique binding and whipping properties previously only seen in egg whites. Different brands will yield slightly different results, but I've never found any that are complete duds. For more delicate applications like meringues or marshmallow fluff, you can always concentrate your aquafaba to create a stronger foam matrix by cooking it gently over the stove and reducing some of the water.

Arrowroot Powder/Flour

Thanks to arrowroot, you can thicken sauces, puddings, and mousses with ease. This white powder is very similar to kudzu and is often compared to other starchy flours. However, arrowroot is so fine that it produces much smoother, creamier results, and is less likely to stick together and form large lumps. It also thickens liquids much more quickly than cornstarch or potato starch, without leaving an unpleasant, raw sort of cereal flavor behind.

Black Salt (Kala Namak)

Lovingly if crudely nicknamed "fart salt" in my household, the sulfurous odor released by a big bagful really does smell like . . . well, you can probably guess. Despite that unpromising introduction, it does taste far better, and eerily similar to eggs. Enhancing everything from tofu scrambles to loaves of challah, it's one of those secret ingredients that every vegan should have in their arsenal. Don't let the name confuse you though; the fine grains are actually mottled pink in appearance, not black.

Bragg Liquid Aminos

Made from soybeans and closely resembling traditional soy sauce in both flavor and color, the two can be swapped at a 1:1 ratio if you should ever find your pantry lacking for either. There are very subtle nuances differentiating the taste of the two, making the liquid aminos slightly sweeter and savory in a way that I believe mimics fish sauce more closely. For those with soy sensitivities there are also coconut-based liquid aminos that can be purchased at health food stores or high-end specialty grocers.

Butter

It's a basic kitchen staple, but good dairy-free butter can be quite elusive if you don't know what to look for. Some name brands contain whey or other milk-derivatives, while others conceal the elusive, animal-derived vitamin D3, so be alert when scanning ingredient labels. For ease, I prefer to use it in stick format, such as Earth Balance® Buttery Sticks or Miyoko's Kitchen European Style Cultured VeganButter. Never try to substitute spreadable margarine butter from a tub! These varieties have much more water to allow them to spread while cold, and will thus bake and cook differently. I always use unsalted margarine butter unless otherwise noted, but you are welcome to use salted as long as you remove about ¼ teaspoon of salt per ¼ cup of butter from the recipe. Overly salted food is one of the first flaws that diners notice, so take care with your seasoning and always adjust to taste.

Cacao Nibs

Also known as raw chocolate, cacao nibs are unprocessed cacao nuts, simply broken up into smaller pieces. Considerably more earthy and harsh than the sweet, mellow chocolate found in bars or chips, it is often used for texture and accent flavor in desserts. Sometimes it can be found coated in sugar to soften its inherent bitter edge, but for baking or cooking, you'll want to start with the plain, raw version for the most versatility. Seek out bags of cacao nibs in health food stores; if you're really lucky, you may be able to find them in the bulk bins of well-stocked specialty stores.

Chia Seeds

Yes, this is the same stuff that makes chia pets so green and fuzzy, and yes, the seeds are edible! Tiny but mighty, what makes these particular seeds so special is that they form a gel when mixed with liquid. This makes them a powerful binder when trying to replace eggs, or should flaxseeds be in short supply. Store in the freezer for a longer lifespan, and grind them before using in baked goods to maintain an even crumb texture.

Chocolate

Chocolate is chocolate, right? Oh, if only it were so simple. Needless to say, conventional white and milk chocolate are out of the picture, but some so-called dark chocolates still don't make the dairy-free cut. Even those that claim to be "70% cacao solids, extra-special dark" may have milk solids or butterfat lurking within. Don't buy the hype or the fillers! Stay vigilant and check labels for milk-based ingredients, as unadulterated chocolate is far superior. Semi-sweet has approximately half as much sugar as cocoa solids, and bittersweet tends to have even less. Baker's chocolate is always vegan and entirely unsweetened, so it has intense chocolate flavor, but isn't the tastiest option for eating out of hand. Dark chocolate is somewhat of a catch-all term that has no official nor legal definition.

Coconut Milk

When called for in this book, I'm referring to regular, full-fat coconut milk. That fat is necessary for creating a smooth, creamy mouth feel, and of course a richer taste. Light coconut milk or coconut milk beverages found in aseptic containers may be suitable in some cases for particularly calorie-conscious cooks, but such a substitution is likely to have detrimental effects on the overall texture of the dish. For best results, treat yourself to the genuine article. Plain coconut milk is found canned in the ethnic foods aisle of the grocery store. You can make it yourself from fresh coconut meat, but in most cases, the added hassle honestly isn't worth the expense or effort.

Coconut Oil

Once demonized as artery-clogging sludge not fit to grease a doorframe, nutritionists now can't recommend this tropical fat highly enough. Touted for its benefits when consumed or used on the skin or hair, it's readily available just about anywhere you turn. Two varieties populate store shelves: Virgin (also labeled as raw or unrefined) coconut oil and refined coconut oil. Virgin gets the best press from the health experts since it's less processed, and it bears the subtle aroma of the coconut flesh. Refined is wonderful for baked goods, however, since it has been deodorized and is essentially flavorless, allowing it to blend seamlessly into any dish. They both solidify below 76°F, but virgin oil reaches its smoke point at 350°F while refined is at 450°F, meaning you can safely use it to fry or roast food at much higher temperatures. Either works fine for raw or unbaked applications, so feel free to choose either one based on how much you want to taste the coconut essence in the final product.

Cocoa Butter

Chocolate is comprised of two key elements: The cocoa solids, which give it that distinct cocoa flavor, and the cocoa butter, which is the fat that provides the body. Cocoa butter is solid at room temperature, like all tropical oils, so it's best to measure it after melting, as the firm chunks can appear deceptively voluminous. It's important to pick up high-quality, food-grade cocoa butter. As a popular ingredient in body lotions and lip balms, some offerings come with fillers and undesirable additives, so shop carefully if you search locally. Avoid deodorized cocoa butter, unless you'd rather omit its natural flavor from your desserts.

Confectioners' Sugar

Otherwise known as powdered sugar, icing sugar, or 10x sugar, confectioners' sugar is a very finely ground version of standard white sugar, often with a touch of starch included to prevent clumping. You can make your own by powdering 1 cup of granulated sugar with 1 tablespoon of cornstarch in your food processor or spice grinder. Simply blend on the highest speed for about two minutes, allowing the dust to settle before opening your machine—unless you want to inhale a cloud of sugar!

Cream Cheese

Many innovative companies now make dairy-free products that will give you the most authentic shmears and cream cheese frostings imaginable. These soft spreads also hold up beautifully in cookie dough and piecrusts, contributing a great tangy flavor and excellent structure. My favorite brand is the classic Tofutti®, but there are now numerous options available that all work just as well in dessert applications. This ingredient is hard to replace with homemade varieties when seeking smooth, consistent results, so I suggest that you check out your local mega-mart or natural food grocer, or head online if all else fails.

Dehydrated Onion Flakes

Want to know the secret to what makes everything bagels so great? Dehydrated onion flakes. Yes, it's a careful balance of many delightful seeds and seasonings, but the dried onions are what really carry the whole flavor. You might be forgiven for cutting back on any other single component, whereas an allium deficit would throw the entire balance into unrecognizable disarray. Most supermarkets and specialty spice shops such as Penzeys or MySpiceSage.com can accommodate, with the option of toasted onion flakes as well, lending a warmer, roasted note to the blend. You can make your own if you have a dehydrator, or a slow oven and a lot of patience. Just dice two or three onions and spread them out on a non-stick tray or silpat. Dehydrate for 4 to 10 hours, or bake in the oven using at the lowest setting possible (usually around 160–170°F) for 3 to 8 hours, stirring periodically, until crisp and papery.

Five-Spice Powder

A powerful mixture of anise, pepper, cinnamon, fennel seed, and cloves, we owe Chinese cuisine for this spicy representation of the five basic tastes—salty, sweet, sour, bitter, and savory. Ratios and exact blends vary depending on who you ask, and every cook seems to have their own family recipe, so go ahead and tweak until it pleases your own palate. Most grocery stores will stock the seasoning in the spice aisle, but here's how I like to mix mine up at home:

2 tablespoons ground star anise
2 tablespoons crushed cinnamon stick pieces
2 teaspoons ground fennel seeds
2 teaspoons crushed Szechuan peppercorns
¼ teaspoon ground cloves

Toss all the spices into a coffee or spice grinder, and let the machine pulverize everything to a fine powder. Make sure that there are no large pieces or unmixed pockets of spice before transferring to an airtight jar. Dark-colored glass is the best option, because light will degrade the flavors faster.
If you can't find Szechuan peppercorns, an equal amount of either black or white peppercorns can be substituted for a slightly different but similarly fiery bite.

Flavor Extracts

I usually try to stay as far away from flavor extracts as possible, because they are all too often artificial, insipid, and a poor replacement for the real thing. However, vanilla (see page xxi for further details), peppermint, and almond are my main exceptions, as high-quality extracts from the actual sources are readily available in most markets. Just make sure to avoid any bottles that list sugar, corn syrup, colors, or chemical stabilizers in addition to your flavor of choice.

Flaxseeds

Ground flaxseeds make an excellent vegan egg-replacer when combined with water. One tablespoon of the whole seeds produces approximately 1½ tablespoons of the ground powder. While you can purchase pre-ground flaxseed meal in many stores, I prefer to grind them fresh for each recipe, as they tend to go rancid much more quickly once broken down. Not to mention, it takes mere seconds to powder your own flaxseeds in a spice grinder. If you do opt to purchase flax meal instead, be sure to store the powder in your refrigerator or freezer until you are ready to use it. These tiny seeds can be found in bulk bins and prepackaged in the baking aisle of natural food stores.

Garbanzo Bean (Chickpea) Flour

Gaining in popularity as a versatile gluten-free flour, garbanzo flour is just what you might imagine; nothing but dried, finely ground chickpeas. When used in baking, it can be used as a substitute for about 20 to 25 percent of the wheat flour called for in a recipe or to add a toothsome density to cakes or cookies. It can also be cooked with water like polenta, and eaten either as a hot porridge or let set overnight in a baking dish, sliced, and then fried to make what is called chickpea panisse. Just be warned that eaten raw (if, say, someone decided to sample raw cookie batter that contains garbanzo flour) it is very bitter and unpleasant. Garbanzo flour should be readily available in most grocery stores in the baking or natural foods section, but if you have a powerful blender like a Vitamix with a dry grinding container, you can make your own from dried, split chickpeas (also known as chana dal). Process 2 cups of legumes at a time, and use the plunger to keep things moving. Once finely ground, let the dust settle for a few minutes before removing the lid of the container.

Graham Crackers

When I first went searching for vegan graham crackers, I was appalled at my lack of options. Why every brand in sight needed to include honey was beyond me. So, what is an intrepid food enthusiast to do in a tight situation like this? Shop, search, and browse some more, of course. Concealed among the rest, and often in natural foods stores, there are a few brands that exclude all animal products. Believe it or not, some of the best options are the store-brand, no-name biscuits that may otherwise get overlooked. Keep your eyes peeled for unexpected steals and deals.

Garlic

Quite possibly the single most celebrated seasoning the world over, garlic itself needs no explanation. Such popularity, however, has given rise to a wide range of garlicky options, some better suited for various recipes than others. There's no standard size for a clove of garlic, but a good rule of thumb is that on average, a clove will yield about 1 teaspoon, minced. Granulated or powdered garlic is a bit more concentrated, so you can generally substitute ¼- to ½-teaspoon per clove if you're out of the fresh stuff, or simply want the distinctive flavor without the raw bite. You can also find prepared, already-minced, or pureed garlic both in shelf-stable jars and frozen packets for super-speedy cooking needs.

Granulated Sugar

Yes, plain old, regular white sugar. Surprised to see this basic sweetener here? It's true that all sugar (beet or cane) is derived from plant sources and therefore vegan by nature. However, there are some sneaky things going on behind the scenes in big corporations these days. Some cane sugar is filtered using bone char, a very non-vegan process, but that will never be specified on a label. If you're not sure about the brand that you typically buy, your best bet is to contact the manufacturer directly and ask.

To bypass this problem, many vegans purchase unbleached cane sugar. While it is a suitable substitute, unbleached cane sugar does have a higher molasses content than white sugar, so it has more of a brown sugar–like flavor, and tends to produce desserts that are denser. Luckily, there are a few caring companies that go to great pains to ensure the purity of their sugar products, such as Florida Crystals® and Amalgamated Sugar Company®, the suppliers to White Satin, Fred Meyer, Western Family, and Parade. I typically opt for one of these vegan sugar brands to get the best results. You can often find appropriate sugar in health food store bulk bins these days to save some money, but as always, verify the source before forking over the cash. As sugar can be a touchy vegan subject, it is best to use your own judgment when considering which brand to purchase.

Harissa

Many people refer to this as the North African answer to hot sauce, but this complex red pepper paste is so much more sophisticated than that. A wide variety of chiles are blended together, including but not limited to serrano, bell peppers, bird's eye chiles, and dried, rehydrated chiles such as Arbol, Guallio, chipotle, and ancho peppers, along with more exotic seasonings such as saffron, rosewater, and coriander. This combination lends it an unmistakable, unlimitable spicy perfume. Its closest relative is skhug (otherwise known as shug or zhug), a hot sauce found in Middle Eastern cuisine with similar flavors. You can find jars of harissa either with the other hot sauces at your local specialty market, or amongst the pickled and preserved foods. Luckily, it's also a snap to make at home from the following formula:

1 roasted red bell pepper
3–4 hot chiles of choice (see above for suggestions)
4 cloves garlic
3 tablespoons olive oil
2 tablespoons lemon juice
1 teaspoon salt
½ teaspoon ground caraway
½ teaspoon ground coriander
¼ teaspoon ground cumin
¼ teaspoon rosewater
Pinch saffron (optional)

Simply toss all the ingredients into your food processor or blender and pulse to purée, pausing as needed to scrape down the sides of the bowl to make sure everything is incorporated. Once the paste is smooth, transfer to an airtight glass jar and store in the fridge for up to 3 weeks. You can further extend its shelf life if you pour additional oil right on top, just enough to cover the surface and effectively seal the freshness in.

Hemp Seeds

Yes, these are edible seeds from cannabis sativa, but unlike the leaves, they won't get you high. Instead, they're a concentrated source of omega-3 fatty acids and many other vital nutrients, which has bolstered their public profile in recent years. Dubbed a superfood by many, what I find most attractive about these tiny kernels is their deeply savory, nutty flavor that blends nicely into both sweet and savory applications. Most hemp seeds are sold hulled, to make them a bit easier on the digestion, and are often squirreled away amongst the dietary supplements or in bulk bins.

Instant Coffee Powder or Granules

Though generally unfit for drinking as intended, instant coffee is an ideal way to add those crave-worthy roasted, smoky notes to any recipe without also incorporating a lot of extra liquid. Stored in a dry, dark place, a small jar should last a long time. You can even find decaf versions, in case you're more sensitive to caffeine but still want that flavor in your recipes. I prefer powder to granules because it dissolves more easily, but both can work interchangeably with a bit of vigorous mixing.

Jackfruit

Practically unheard of just a few years ago, jackfruit has taken the world by storm for its uncanny ability to imitate the texture of shredded meat. These tropical fruits can grow to gigantic proportions, easily exceeding eighty pounds, and their spiny exterior makes them quite a sight to behold. You're much more likely to encounter them canned, which is a merciful thing because their latex-y interior is a real pain to break down, coating everything from your knife to your hands in stubbornly sticky goo. Always make sure you're purchasing young (or "immature") green jackfruit in brine, *not* in syrup. The sweetened stuff is objectively dreadful.

Maple Syrup

One of my absolute favorite sweeteners, there is simply no substitute for real, 100 percent maple syrup. The flavor is like nothing else out there, and I have yet to meet a single brand of pancake syrup that could even come close. Of course, this incredible indulgence does come at a hefty price. Though it would be absolute sacrilege to use anything but authentic maple syrup on pancakes or waffles in my house, I will sometimes bend the rules in recipes where it isn't such a prominent flavor, in order to save some money. In these instances, I'll substitute with a maple-agave blend, which still carries the flavor from the actual source, but bulks it up with an equal dose of agave for sweetening power.

Matcha

Perhaps one of my all-time favorite flavorings, matcha is a very high-quality powdered green tea. It is used primarily in Japanese tea ceremonies and can have an intense, complex, and bitter taste when used in large amounts. Contrary to what many new bakers think, this is not the same as the green tea leaves you'll find in mega-mart tea bags! Those are vastly inferior in the flavor department, and real matcha is ground much finer. There are many levels of quality, with each step up in grade carrying a higher price tag. Because it can become quite pricey, I would suggest buying a mid-range or "culinary" grade, which should be readily available at any specialty tea store and many health food markets.

Miso Paste

Fermented soybeans coarsely ground and mixed with water sounds like a sad excuse for soup, yet it's the single most celebrated starter for any Japanese meal, be it breakfast, lunch, or dinner. The length of time that the beans are fermented determines the color and flavor of the finished paste; traditional miso is aged for at least three to five years, yielding a very dark, robust, and salty base. Lighter, gentler miso is often called "sweet" miso, which is delicious used as a condiment as well, spread very thinly on an ear of roasted corn, for example. Those sensitive to soy can now find many alternatives as well, the most common being chickpea miso, which more closely mimics the flavor of a light or white miso paste. Though all types can be substituted with more or less success, no two misos are exactly alike, and any changes can drastically change the end results.

Mochi and Mochiko

Mochiko is simply finely ground mochi flour, or glutinous rice flour. You can find this in any Asian specialty market or online. Koda Farms® is one of the most common brands available in the United States; it can be purchased in compact, white 1-pound boxes. To make your own mochi, it just takes a microwave and a few minutes!

¾ cup mochiko
⅓ cup confectioners' sugar (optional; omit if using in savory dishes)

¾ cup water
½ cup potato starch, tapioca starch, or cornstarch

Place the mochiko in a medium microwave-safe bowl along with the sugar (if using) and water. Whisk vigorously until no lumps remain. Loosely cover the bowl with plastic wrap and microwave for 1 minute. Use a slightly dampened nonstick spatula to stir before re-covering and microwaving for an additional minute. Stir again, cover once more, and microwave for a final 30 seconds. It should be doughy, slightly gelatinous, and almost translucent.

Line a baking sheet with parchment paper and dust generously with your starch of choice. Place the hot mochi on top, cover with additional starch, and let cool until you can comfortably handle it. Use a rolling pin to flatten the ball out to about ¼-inch thickness. Add more starch as needed to prevent it from sticking. Chill the whole sheet for about 10 to 15 minutes, until firm and cool to the touch.

Use a very sharp knife to cut the slab into smaller, bite-sized pieces. Lightly brush away the excess starch. You can use the mochi as an ice cream topper, in soup like little dumplings, or cooked into okonomiyaki (page 50).

Non-Dairy Milk

The foundation of many cream and custard pies, I kept this critical ingredient somewhat ambiguous for a reason. Most types of non-dairy milk will work in these recipes, which leaves the possibilities wide open for anyone that needs to accommodate allergies or intolerances. Unless explicitly specified, any other type of vegan milk-substitute will work. My top pick is unsweetened almond milk because it tends to be a bit thicker, richer, and still has a neutral flavor. Don't be afraid to experiment, though; there's a lot to choose from!

Nori

If you've ever eaten sushi, you're already well acquainted with nori. It's the flat sheet of seaweed wrapped around your rice, so dark green that sometimes it looks black. Nori is easily found in any grocery store that has a section devoted to Asian imports, and most options are equally suitable for all preparations. The whole sheets work well as low-carb wraps beyond the sushi sphere, but they can also be snipped or crumbled into oceanic toppings for ramen, soba noodles, or rice bowls.

Nutritional Yeast

Unlike active yeast, nutritional yeast is not used to leaven baked goods, but to flavor all sorts of dishes. Prized for its distinctly cheesy flavor, it's a staple in most vegan pantries and is finally starting to gain recognition in mainstream cooking as well. Though almost always found in savory recipes, I sometimes like to add a tiny pinch to some desserts, bringing out its subtle buttery characteristics. It can be found either in the baking aisle or in many bulk bin sections.

Panko Bread Crumbs

This Japanese import is much crisper and more airy than so-called "Italian-style" bread crumbs. That unique texture allows it to better resist absorbing oil when fried, yielding lighter, less greasy coatings.

When used as filler or binder within recipes, it has a less prominent wheat flavor, allowing it to blend seamlessly into the background of just about anything, sweet or savory.

Salt

The importance of salt cannot be overstated. It's that spark that makes flavors pop and balances out spice mixtures that might otherwise overwhelm the palate. To make a long story short, you do not want to leave out this unassuming but critical ingredient! Unless otherwise noted, I use regular old table salt (finely ground) in baking. Flaky sea salt or kosher salt can be fun to sprinkle directly over finished baked goods before serving for an extra punch of flavor, but be careful not to overdo it; there's a fine line between salted and downright salty.

Seitan

All hail seitan! No, there's no demon worship going on here, and in fact seitan originated on the opposite end of that spectrum. Buddhist monks first invented this "wheat meat" in ancient China, long before there was even a word for vegetarianism. Seitan is pure gluten, the stuff of celiac nightmares, but of body building dreams. Ounce for ounce, seitan has the same amount of protein as lean ground beef, and of course, less fat and no cholesterol. Textures range from chewy to spongy to pleasantly sinewy, depending on how it's sliced and cooked. Ready to use, prepared seitan can be found in health food stores and Whole Foods Markets alongside the packages of refrigerated tofu.

Sour Cream

Another creative alternative comes to the rescue of vegan eaters everywhere! Vegan sour cream provides an amazingly similar yet dairy-free version of the original tangy spread. In a pinch, I suppose you might be able to get away with using soy yogurt instead, but that is generally much thinner, so I really wouldn't recommend it. Vegan sour cream is sold in the refrigerated section of natural food stores and some mainstream grocers. It can often be found neatly tucked in among its dairy-based rivals, or with the other refrigerated dairy alternatives.

Sprinkles

What's a birthday party without a generous handful of sprinkles to brighten up the cake? Though these colorful toppers are made primarily of edible wax, they are often coated in confectioners' glaze, which is code for mashed up insects, to give them their lustrous shine. Happily, you can now find specifically vegan sprinkles (sold as "sprinkelz") produced by the Let's Do…® company, in both chocolate and colored versions, which can be found at just about any natural food store.

Sriracha

True heat-seekers and hot sauce fanatics may scoff at the relatively mild spice of sriracha, but that very quality is what makes it such a winning condiment for enhancing all cuisines. Leaning more heavily on garlic and a balanced sweetness than just pure fire power, it's dangerously easy to power through even the largest bottles available. Don't hold back, just enjoy the blaze; it's dirt-cheap and found literally everywhere, even in gas stations and truck stops.

Sumac

Ask the internet what it thinks about "sumac" and the first thing to pop up won't be about its culinary value, but about its toxicity. While closely related to poison ivy and sometimes confused with its less-friendly brethren in the wild, dried and ground sumac is an entirely different beast. Contributing the pucker-power of a lemon with punchy sourness and astringency, it has the benefit of being a powdered seasoning that won't water down your dishes. For a reasonable stand-in, blend lemon zest with a pinch of salt, but don't expect the exact same results.

Tahini

An irreplaceable staple in Middle Eastern cuisine, most regular grocery stores should be able to accommodate your tahini requests. Tahini is a paste very much like peanut butter, but made from sesame seeds rather than nuts. If you don't have any on hand and a trip to the market is not in your immediate plans, then any other nut butter will provide exactly the same texture within a recipe, though it will impart a different overall taste. You can also make your own, just like you would make nut butter, but a high-speed blender is highly recommended to achieve a smooth texture.

Tamarind Paste

Tangy, tart, and often downright sour, tamarind possesses a powerful, sometimes polarizing flavor that's best used sparingly to balance out a dish, rather than dominate. Harvesting the edible fruit from the pod can be a taxing proposition, thanks to its tough outer shell, fibrous interior, and hard, sticky seeds. Head straight for the prepared paste, a smooth, soft puree, to bypass the labor without sacrificing the taste. It's readily available anywhere that exotic fruits are sold, either in the fresh produce section or canned goods aisle. Stored in an airtight container in the fridge, I've found that it's pretty much indestructible.

Tapioca Flour/Starch

Tapioca isn't just for pudding anymore! This gluten-free go-to has made great gains as a versatile ingredient in sweet and savory cooking in recent years, but confusion remains about what exactly it is. Made from the cassava root, the terms "flour" and "starch" can be used interchangeably depending on the manufacturer. Ultimately, it's all the same stuff, perfect for thickening stews, creating a crispy coating, and so much more. In a pinch, an equal measure of potato starch or arrowroot can be substituted.

Tempeh

Tempeh is often compared to tofu because it's another high-protein soy product, but that's pretty much where the similarities end. Much more strongly flavored than tofu, tempeh is made from whole beans, and sometimes grains and even seeds, which are bound together in a fermented cake. Good bacteria cultures like those found in yogurt are the catalyst for this slow transformation, which makes it particularly high in B12 and beneficial for gut health. Raw tempeh can be somewhat bitter which is why it's best cooked over high heat with equally assertive marinades. Although there are many different varieties available, they can all be used interchangeably.

Tofu

No longer the posterchild for flavorless vegetarian cookery, tofu is enjoying greater acceptance than ever as a highly versatile protein in its own right, rather than merely a bland meat substitute. For entrees where the tofu is chopped, sliced, or cubed, you should seek out firm, extra-firm, or even super-firm, water-packed varieties than can hold their own when the heat is on. Medium or firm are better for crumbled applications, and soft or silken is most appropriate for creamy purees, such as sauces, smoothies, and puddings. When I use tofu for baked goods and ice creams, I always reach for the aseptic, shelf-stable packs. Not only do they seem to last forever when unopened, but they also blend down into a perfectly smooth liquid when processed thoroughly, not a trace of grit or off-flavors to be found. Water-packed varieties can be stored for up to a month unopened, or one week if stored in an airtight container in the fridge, covered in fresh water that's changed every two or three days.

Vanilla (Extract, Paste, and Beans)

One of the most important ingredients in a baker's arsenal, vanilla is found in countless forms and qualities. It goes without saying that artificial flavorings pale in comparison to the real thing. Madagascar vanilla is the traditional full-bodied vanilla that most people appreciate in desserts, so stick with that and you can't go wrong. Happily, it's also the most common and moderately priced variety. To take your desserts up a step, vanilla paste brings in the same amount of flavor, but includes those lovely little vanilla bean flecks that makes everyone think you busted out the good stuff and used whole beans. Vanilla paste can be substituted 1:1 for vanilla extract. Like whole vanilla beans, save the paste for things where you'll really see those specks of vanilla goodness, like ice creams, custards, and frostings. Vanilla beans, the most costly but flavorful option, can be used instead, at about 1 bean per 2 teaspoons of extract or paste.Once you've split and scraped out the insides, don't toss that vanilla pod! Get the most for your money by stashing it in a container of granulated sugar, to slowly infuse the sugar with delicious vanilla flavor. Alternately, just store the pod in a container until it dries out, and then grind it up very finely in a high-speed blender and use it to augment a good vanilla extract. The flavor won't be nearly as strong as the seeds, but it does contribute to the illusion that you've used the good stuff.

Vegetable Stock

Be it brothy or creamy, thick or thin, a soup is only as good as its stock. Stock can be made up of absolutely any vegetables, but the most common ingredients are onions, carrots, and celery, at bare minimum. The trouble with commercial, ready-made options are that most lean too heavily on salt, throwing the carefully-balanced seasoning of a dish out of whack. Always seek out low-sodium or no-salted-added varieties whenever possible, and read labels carefully to avoid artificial flavorings or preservatives. My favorite pantry staple is actual dry vegetable stock powder, which can be added to water according to taste. The best vegetable stock will always be homemade, though. If you have some extra time and some scraps, it's effortless to whip up and then freeze for later use. These aren't set rules, only guidelines, so never feel constrained to any particular measurements if you come up shy or just want to experiment.

2 cups chopped alliums (onions, shallots, leeks, and/or scallions)
2 cups chopped root vegetables (carrots, sweet potatoes, and/or turnips)

1 cup chopped celery or fennel
1 bay leaf
1 teaspoon whole black peppercorns
Salt, to taste

Additional options: garlic, pumpkin, tomatoes, mushrooms, fresh parsley, dried thyme, turmeric
Toss all the ingredients, except for the salt, into a large stock pot, and add just enough water to cover the vegetables. Bring to a boil, cover, and then turn down the heat to keep the liquid at a gentle simmer. Let cook for anywhere between 1 to 2 hours, bearing in mind that the longer you can wait, the more flavor you can extract. Strain out the vegetable solids, saving them either for a puree, soup, or simply compost, and season the golden-brown stock with salt, to taste. Use right away or let cool, transfer into airtight containers, and store in either the fridge or freezer. The stock will keep for up to a week in the fridge, and for up to 4 months in the freezer.

Vinegar

At any given time, there are at least five different types of vinegar kicking around my kitchen, and that's a conservative estimate. As with oil, vinegar can be made from all sorts of fruit, grains, and roots, each with their own distinctive twang. Some, like white vinegar, rice vinegar, and apple cider vinegar are fairly neutral and mild, others like balsamic vinegar and red wine vinegar are far more assertive. The type you choose can radically change the character of the finished dish, which is why they all have a place in my pantry. Feel free to experiment with different varieties for a change of pace if you're open to new flavor adventures. In a pinch, you might also be able to get away with using fresh lemon or lime juice for a similar acidic punch.

Wasabi Paste and Powder

Just like the mounds of green paste served with sushi, the prepared wasabi paste found in tubes is almost certainly not made of wasabi root. Strange but true, it's typically colored horseradish instead, due to the rarity and expense of real wasabi. Read labels carefully, because it's one of those things that seems guaranteed to be vegan-friendly, but can give you a nasty surprise if you're not careful. Milk derivatives are often added, for reasons I couldn't begin to explain. Wasabi powder can be potent stuff indeed, but only if it's extremely fresh. The flavor dissipates over time, so be sure to toss any that has been sitting in your pantry well past its prime. If quality paste is nowhere to be found, opt for prepared horseradish (blended only with a dash of vinegar) instead. In some cases, mustard powder can lend a similar flavor instead of wasabi powder, but only in very small doses.

Whipped Cream

Ready-to-use aerosol cans of vegan whipped cream are hidden in plain sight, right alongside their dairy-based counterparts. Made by Reddi-wip®, it can be found in both coconut- and almond-based versions, and sprays out fluffy and lightly sweetened every time. So Delicious® also offers a frozen whipped topping alternative as well, which needs only to thaw in the fridge before it can be generously dolloped on all manner of sweet treats. You can easily make your own from scratch as well; all you need is a can of full-fat coconut milk and a bit of patience. Place the whole, unopened can in the fridge and let it chill for at least 3 hours. This will allow the cream to rise to the top and solidify, which you can then skim off in thick spoonfuls. Leave the watery refuse behind for another recipe (it's great in curries and soups!). Place the coconut cream in the bowl of your stand mixer, and whip vigorously for 5 to 8 minutes, until thick, fluffy, and luscious. Sprinkle in a touch of sugar and a few drops of vanilla extract, if desired.

White Whole Wheat Flour

Move over whole wheat pastry flour, healthy bakers everywhere have a new best friend! It may look and taste like regular white flour, but it's actually milled from the whole grain. Simply made from hard white wheat berries instead of red, the color and flavor are much lighter, making it the perfect addition to nearly every sort of baking application you can think of. If you're concerned about getting more fiber into your diet, feel free to switch out the all-purpose flour in any recipe in this book for white whole wheat.

Wine

If your wine isn't something you'd want in a glass, it's not something you'd want to cook or bake with, either. Avoid so-called "cooking wines" and just go with something moderately priced, and on the drier side for a savory dish or something a bit sweeter to compliment a dessert. Don't be afraid to ask for help when you go shopping; the people who work at wine stores tend to have good advice about these things! Be vigilant and do your homework though, because not all wines are vegan. Shockingly, some are filtered through isinglass, which is made from fish bladders. To avoid a fishy brew, double check brands on Barnivore.com.

Yogurt

Fermented by good bacteria that are said to improve your digestion, yogurt now comes in just about any flavor, color, or non-dairy formulation you can imagine. Soy, almond, coconut, and even cashew yogurts are readily available at most markets these days, and you can even find some that are aga-ve-sweetened, too. Just double-check that whatever you decide to buy is certified as vegan; just because it's non-dairy doesn't mean it uses vegan cultures. The big, multi-serving tubs are handy if you eat a lot of the stuff to begin with, but I generally prefer to purchase single-serving, 6-ounce containers for specific uses to avoid leftovers that may go bad too soon. Please note, however, that one container of yogurt does not equal one cup; 6 ounces will be equivalent to about ¾ cup by volume measure. It does help to have a food scale if you decide to buy in bulk to weigh out the exact amount that would be found in one standard container.

Young Thai Coconuts

Just as the name might suggest, young Thai coconuts are sold earlier than the iconic, brown-husked versions. The white shell on these immature fruits is much easier to penetrate with your kitchen knife and a few solid whacks, revealing a generous pool of sweet water and soft flesh within. The "meat" is easily scooped out with a sturdy spoon and typically enjoyed raw. Young Thai coconuts are found refrigerated in the produce section of many health food stores, but you can find much better deals at any Asian market.

BREAKFAST

APPLE-CINNAMON PEANUT BUTTER BOSTOCK

MAKES 8 TO 12 SERVINGS

When plain old French toast won't cut it, up the ante with a rich frangipane topping. Bostock is classically made with almond paste slathered over stale brioche, though peanut butter gives my unconventional version a distinctly American accent. Thick like soft, pillowy custard, this lightly spiced topping cradles tender apple slices over each slice of lightly soaked, apple-infused bread. Decadent enough to enjoy as dessert, it's an ideal indulgence for celebratory breakfasts and brunches.

PEANUT BUTTER FRANGIPANE:

½ cup water
2 tablespoons ground flaxseeds
1 cup granulated sugar
1 cup unsweetened creamy peanut
   butter
½ cup vegan butter
1 teaspoon ground cinnamon
1 teaspoon vanilla extract
¼ teaspoon salt

TO ASSEMBLE:

1 (12-ounce) package frozen no sugar-
   added apple juice concentrate,
   thawed
1 loaf (1 pound) French or country
   bread, cut into 1–1½-inch-thick
   slices
2 small apples, cored and thinly sliced
1 cup roasted, unsalted peanuts,
   roughly chopped

Preheat your oven to 375°F and line a half sheet pan with parchment paper or a silicone baking mat; set aside.

To make the peanut butter frangipane, begin by whisking together the water and flaxseeds in a small dish. Allow 15 to 30 minutes for the mixture to thicken into a gel. Hasten the process by microwaving for 30 to 60 seconds if you can't bear to wait.

In the bowl of your stand mixer, combine the sugar, peanut butter, vegan butter, cinnamon, vanilla, and salt. Mix vigorously with the paddle attachment before adding the flax gel. Pause periodically, scraping down the sides of the bowl with a spatula as needed to incorporate all the ingredients. Beat until smooth, somewhere between the consistency of stiff icing and runny frosting.

Pour the apple juice concentrate into a large bowl. Working with one slice at a time, dip each slice of bread in the juice, holding it there for just 3 to 5 seconds to saturate. Squeeze gently to drain the excess liquid, without completely wringing out the bread. Place on the sheet pan, lining slices up so that they're close enough to touch but not overlap. Spread each piece with 3 to 4 tablespoons of the peanut butter mixture, top with a few thin slices of apple, and finish with about 2 tablespoons of chopped peanuts.

Bake until the frangipane has set, the peanuts are toasted, and the edges of the toast have begun to caramelize; about 22 to 25 minutes. Serve warm or let cool and store in an airtight container in the fridge for up to 5 days.

BANANA SHEET PAN CAKES

MAKES 15 TO 20 PANCAKES; 5 TO 6 SERVINGS

Pancakes are a brunch favorite but making them for a crowd is no easy feat. Even with a large skillet or griddle, it's almost impossible to serve everyone a warm short stack at once. Our solution? These easy sheet pan pancakes—essentially a giant, fluffy, buttery pancake that you'll cut into squares and serve warm to friends and family. To achieve the signature golden brown color, we brushed the pancake with melted butter after baking and popped it under the broiler for the finishing touch. Keep it classic with the basic recipe or try one of our variations below. No matter your add-ins, be sure to serve with butter and maple syrup.

3 very ripe, large bananas, divided
2 cups plain non-dairy milk
1 tablespoon apple cider vinegar
½ teaspoon vanilla extract
¼ cup vegan butter or coconut oil, melted and divided
2½ cups all-purpose flour
3 tablespoons granulated sugar
1 tablespoon baking powder
1 teaspoon baking soda
½ teaspoon salt
¼ cup chocolate chips, chopped nuts, or sliced strawberries (optional)

Preheat your oven to 400°F and lightly grease a half sheet pan.

In a medium bowl, vigorously mash two of the bananas until fairly smooth. Mix in the non-dairy milk, vinegar, vanilla, and 3 tablespoons of the melted vegan butter or coconut oil. Stir until fully incorporated.

Separately, in a large bowl, whisk together the flour, sugar, baking powder, baking soda, and salt. Pour the liquid mixture into the bowl of dry goods and use a wide spatula to combine. Stir until the batter is just blended; a few lumps are perfectly fine, and in fact encouraged! Over-mixing is the mortal enemy of tender, fluffy pancakes.

Pour the pancake batter onto your prepared sheet pan, spreading it evenly to reach all the sides in one smooth layer. Slice the remaining banana and sprinkle the rounds across the top, followed by any other goodies you'd like to include.

Bake for 15 minutes until golden brown around the edges. Brush with remaining vegan butter or coconut oil, turn on the broil to high, and cook for an additional 5 minutes to give the top a fetching golden tan.

Cool for at least 5 minutes before slicing and stacking up.

BLACK BEAN CHILAQUILES

MAKES 2 SERVINGS

South of the border, chilaquiles have been an essential staple for using up stale tortilla chips but take on greater flavor when prepared fresh, from scratch. Homemade corn tortilla chips are baked and not fried in this healthy take on breakfast nachos. Little prep or planning is needed to throw together fresh salsa, black beans, and smashed avocado in a meal that can be scaled for one or one dozen.

CHILAQUILES:

4 (6-inch) corn tortillas
1 tablespoon olive oil
¼ cup diced red onion
1 clove garlic, minced
2 large tomatoes, diced (about 2 cups)
1 cup cooked black beans
2 tablespoons pickled jalapeños, minced
½ teaspoon ground cumin
½ teaspoon chipotle powder
¼ teaspoon dried oregano
¼ teaspoon salt
⅛ teaspoon ground black pepper
2 tablespoons pepitas (shelled pumpkin seeds)
¼ cup fresh cilantro

BASIC GUACAMOLE:

1 medium, ripe avocado, diced
1–2 tablespoons lime juice
¼ teaspoon salt

Preheat your oven to 350°F. Slice the tortillas into sixths or eighths to make neat, equal triangles. Toss with the olive oil to coat and spread the pieces out in an even layer across two half sheet pans without overlapping. Bake for 10 to 15 minutes, until golden brown and crisp.

Meanwhile, prepare the salsa by combining the onion, garlic, tomatoes, black beans, jalapeño, cumin, chipotle powder, oregano, salt, and pepper in a medium bowl. Stir well to incorporate.

Top the baked tortilla chips with equal amounts of the salsa and sprinkle with pepitas. Bake for just 5 more minutes to slightly soften the tortillas and warm through.

While it finishes baking, mash together the avocado, lime juice, and salt in a small bowl. Adjust the seasoning to taste.

Transfer to plates or eat right out of the sheet pans. Top the chilaquiles with fresh cilantro and dollops of guacamole. Serve hot.

> **In a rush?** Replace the tortillas with 4 ounces of tortilla chips to skip the initial baking. You can use approximately 2 cups of your favorite salsa instead of the tomatoes, jalapeños, and spices to cut down on all the chopping, too.

CINNAMON SUGAR SWEET POTATOAST

MAKES 2 TO 4 SERVINGS

Calling it "toast" is a bit of a stretch, I'll admit, but it's the concept that counts. No bread need apply for this vegetable-based quick fix. Thin planks of buttery sweet potato get a light kiss of heat from the oven for a crispy exterior and tender center. Lightly sprinkled with cinnamon sugar, the top layer caramelizes almost like crème brûlée, yielding to the fork with a crisp, crackling snap. Dress it up or down by sticking with the basics or adding whipped coconut cream, chopped nuts, or any fresh fruits your heart desires.

2 medium sweet potatoes
1 tablespoon olive oil
2 tablespoons coconut sugar or dark
    brown sugar, firmly packed
½ teaspoon ground cinnamon
⅛ teaspoon salt
1 banana, sliced (optional)
2 tablespoons chopped pecans
    (optional)

Preheat your oven to 400°F.

Begin by thoroughly scrubbing your sweet potatoes, or peeling if you're not a fan of the skins. Slice lengthwise into ¼-inch thick planks using a very sharp knife or mandoline. Go slowly to ensure consistency, and to be careful as the potatoes may try to roll away from you!

In a large bowl, whisk together the oil, sugar, cinnamon, and salt. Add the sliced sweet potatoes and gently toss to coat.

Transfer to a 13 × 18-inch sheet pan, spreading the pieces out in one even layer, without overlapping. Bake for 15 minutes before flipping. Roast for another 10 to 15 minutes, until caramelized and golden brown all over. Let cool for at least 5 minutes.

Top with sliced bananas and chopped pecans, if desired. Enjoy warm!

> **Your pantry is the limit when it comes to creative toppings. Try lavishing your toasted taters with a drizzle of almond butter, maple syrup, or even toasted vegan marshmallows, too.**

CONFETTI CAKE GRANOLA

MAKES ABOUT 6 CUPS; 6 TO 12 SERVINGS

Getting older means that I'm adult enough to choose a slice of fluffy, frosted vanilla cake as part of a balanced breakfast. It also means that I'm wise enough to opt for something else 364 days of the year. For all those unbirthdays, it's perfectly reasonable to indulge in this birthday cake granola instead. It has all the buttery sweetness and rainbow sprinkles, with a considerably more substantial serving of fiber, at least. Feel free to double the batch to always have some on hand, because every morning should be worth celebrating, right?

3 cups crispy rice cereal
3 cups old-fashioned rolled oats
1 cup granulated sugar
½ cup cake flour
½ cup vegan butter, melted
2 tablespoons maple syrup
1½ teaspoons vanilla extract
¼ teaspoon salt
½ cup vegan white chocolate chips or chunks
¼ cup rainbow sprinkles

Preheat your oven to 325°F and line a half sheet pan with aluminum foil or parchment.

In a large bowl, stir together the rice cereal, oats, sugar, and flour. Drizzle the melted butter, maple syrup, and vanilla on top. Add the salt and stir vigorously to combine and thoroughly coat all the grains.

Transfer the mixture to your prepared sheet pan, spreading it out into as thin a layer as possible.

Bake for 30 to 45 minutes, stirring every 15 minutes, until golden brown all over. It will continue to crisp as it cools.

Let cool completely before adding the white chocolate and sprinkles, tossing to distribute the goodies throughout. Store in a cool place in an airtight container for up to two weeks.

> **Will you break the recipe if you use all-purpose flour instead of cake flour? No, no you won't. You'll just be missing out on some of the fine nuances that make this scream *cake* instead of *oats*. It will still taste like a party in your mouth.**
>
> **If it's not your kind of party without bittersweet chocolate, feel free to swap out the white morsels for some of the darker stuff.**

DENVER OMELET ROULADE

MAKES 10 TO 12 SERVINGS

No greasy spoon diner would be complete without a Denver omelet on the menu. Loaded with diced ham, peppers, and onions, it's the American answer to the dainty French staple. For that same satisfying flavor sensation, don't spend your morning flipping over the stove to feed a crowd; wake and bake to turn out a show-stopping savory roulade. Made from a sturdy chickpea base, sweet and smoky cubes of marinated tofu make this a protein-packed entrée to satisfy the most monstrous of appetites. Lightly caramelized around the edges, creamy on the inside, the average eggless omelet has nothing on this savory spiral.

TOFU HAM:

½ cup pineapple juice
¼ cup maple syrup
2 tablespoons soy sauce
2 teaspoons Dijon mustard
½ teaspoon liquid smoke
⅛ teaspoon ground cloves
½ pound extra-firm tofu, cut into ¼-inch cubes

CHICKPEA OMELET:

½ medium yellow onion, diced
½ medium red bell pepper, diced
1 (4-ounce) can diced hatch chilies, drained
1½ cups chickpea flour
3 tablespoons nutritional yeast
3 tablespoons ground flaxseeds
1 tablespoon tapioca flour
1 teaspoon onion powder
1½ teaspoons black salt (kala namak)
½ teaspoon baking powder
½ teaspoon turmeric
4 cups water

TO ASSEMBLE:

1 (8-ounce) package vegan cream cheese, softened

Preheat your oven to 350°F. Line a half sheet pan with aluminum foil or parchment paper and lightly grease; set aside.

In a small bowl, whisk together the pineapple juice, maple syrup, soy sauce, mustard, liquid smoke, and cloves. Add the tofu and toss to coat, making sure it's fully submerged in the liquid. Let stand at room temperature for 30 to 60 minutes to marinate, or speed up the process by microwaving for 2 to 3 minutes. Drain and discard or reserve the excess marinade for another recipe.

Scatter the tofu evenly over the prepared sheet pan along with the diced onion, bell pepper, and hatch chilies. Bake for 20 minutes, stirring halfway through.

Meanwhile, in a large bowl, whisk together the chickpea flour, nutritional yeast, flaxseeds, tapioca flour, onion powder, black salt, baking powder, and turmeric. Once the mixture is homogenous, slowly pour the water into the dry ingredients, whisking until smooth. Make sure there are no lumps before proceeding.

Pour the omelet batter into the pan, evenly covering the tofu and vegetables. Gently tap the pan a few times on the counter to release any air bubbles.

Bake for 20 minutes until the batter has set and is slightly pulling away from the sides.

Let cool for 15 minutes before spreading evenly with cream cheese. Use the edges of the foil or parchment paper as a sling to gently lift the omelet out of the pan. Roll the omelet lengthwise, from short end to short end, peeling away the foil or paper as you go. Be very gentle, as it can be a bit fragile.

Cut into 10 to 12 pieces and serve warm. It's stunning all by itself, but also fantastic on a toasted bagel or English muffin.

If your omelet breaks in the middle of rolling, don't fret! Embrace a more freeform meal, cut it up into random pieces, and just call it a scramble.

For a quick fix, feel free to replace the marinated tofu with diced meatless bacon, deli slices, or even breakfast sausages.

FROSTED CORN FLAKES

MAKES 3 TO 6 SERVINGS

Making cereal from scratch takes considerably more dedication than grabbing a box from the pantry but is an incredibly gratifying exercise in DIY food fabrication. By building your bowl from the ground up, you have complete control over every single component. Want organic, quality corn with no fillers or preservatives? Done and done! Further customize to your tastes by experimenting with alternate sweeteners, such as coconut sugar, spice things up with cinnamon or ginger, and play around with blue cornmeal for more colorful crunchy flakes. The most important ingredient here is patience, so plan ahead to have breakfast on the table at a reasonable hour.

1½ cups coarsely ground yellow cornmeal, divided
¼ cup granulated sugar, divided
2 tablespoons cornstarch
¼ teaspoon salt
¾ cup water

Preheat your oven to 350°F and line two half sheet pans with parchment paper or silicone baking mats.

In a large bowl, whisk together 1 cup of the cornmeal, 1 tablespoon of the sugar, cornstarch, salt, and water. The resulting batter should be thin and somewhat soupy, almost like a melted milkshake.

Divide the batter equally between the two sheet pans, spreading it out in as thin a layer as possible. Don't worry about getting a flush fill that reaches all the way to the edges; the overall shape isn't important.

Whisk together the remaining cornmeal and sugar in a small bowl. Sprinkle the mixture over the top of both sheets.

Bake on the center rack for about 15 minutes. The cornmeal sheets should dry out and form small cracks throughout. Rotate the pans, and reduce the heat to 250°F. Bake for another 15 minutes, until lightly golden around the edges.

Remove the pans from the oven, let rest until cool enough to handle, and break into small flakes. Return the pieces to the oven for just 5 to 10 minutes longer to ensure they're gently toasted and fully crisp all the way through.

Let cool completely before serving or storing in an airtight container.

OATMEAL COOKIE BAKED OATMEAL

MAKES 8 TO 12 SERVINGS

Falling somewhere between buttery oatmeal cookie and wholesome hot cereal, baked oatmeal is really the best of both worlds. Perfect for make-ahead meals, it can be enjoyed warm or cold, plain or dressed up, and satisfies the sweet tooth without blowing your whole day's caloric budget before noon. Plump raisins are embedded between strata of thick cut oats, infused with warming cinnamon throughout. Brown sugar evokes the bakery inspiration for this bowl, while maintaining balance with a good pinch of salt. While I can fully endorse eating cookies for breakfast, this is a more reasonable everyday indulgence.

4 cups old-fashioned rolled oats
1 cup raisins
½ cup blanched almond meal or flour
1 tablespoon ground flaxseeds
1 tablespoon ground cinnamon
2 teaspoons baking powder
1 teaspoon salt
4 cups plain non-dairy milk
1 cup unsweetened applesauce
½ cup dark brown sugar, firmly
    packed
¼ cup vegan butter or coconut oil,
    melted
1½ teaspoons vanilla extract
⅛ teaspoon almond extract

Preheat your oven to 350°F and line a half sheet pan with aluminum foil. Lightly grease and set aside.

In a large bowl, mix the oats, raisins, almond meal, flaxseeds, cinnamon, baking powder, and salt, stirring until well combined.

Separately, combine the non-dairy milk, apple sauce, brown sugar, melted butter, vanilla, and almond extract until smooth. Pour this liquid mix into the bowl of oats, stirring to thoroughly incorporate. Let the mixture sit in the bowl to absorb a bit while the oven finishes coming up to temperature.

Spoon the soupy oat mixture into your prepared sheet pan, spreading it out into an even layer using your spatula. Make sure the raisins are distributed and the oats reach all the sides and corners.

Bake for 30 to 40 minutes, until golden on top and all the liquid has absorbed.

Let cool for at least 15 minutes before slicing or scooping into bowls. If you'd prefer neater squares, wait a bit longer for the oats to set, or chill before reheating in the microwave, as needed. Serve either hot or cold, with additional non-dairy milk if desired.

SPIRALIZED HASH BROWNS

MAKES 6 SERVINGS

Crispy, golden-brown potatoes are always irresistible, but difficult to achieve when serving a crowd. Make easy work of the task by spiralizing instead of shredding your spuds and baking the resulting strands in the oven to achieve perfect results every time.

1½ pounds russet potatoes, well-scrubbed but unpeeled
½ medium yellow onion, thinly sliced
3 tablespoons coconut oil, melted
½ teaspoon salt
½ teaspoon ground black pepper

Preheat your oven to 400°F.

Run the potatoes through the spiralizer, discarding the cylindrical "cores" or saving them for another recipe. Gently rinse in cold water to remove some of the excess starch. This will help ensure crispiness after a trip through the oven. Blot lightly with a paper towel to dry.

Toss the spiralized potatoes together with the onion, coconut oil, salt, and pepper. Make sure that all the potatoes are thoroughly coated, and the onions are well distributed throughout. Transfer to a half sheet pan, spreading the mixture out as evenly as possible.

Bake for 15 minutes before rotating the pan but *do not* stir or flip the potatoes. Bake for another 15 minutes and rotate once more. Continue to bake for about 10 to 15 minutes longer, until perfectly golden-brown on top. Serve immediately, while piping hot and shatteringly crisp.

SUNRISE SCRAMBLE SANDWICH

MAKES 4 SERVINGS

Before daybreak, while the world is still quiet, night owls still wrapped tightly in their beds, my favorite time is that fleeting moment before daybreak, when light filters through the windows anew. A quiet moment of contemplation undisturbed by the usual noise and hustle of the day, watching the sunrise is as revitalizing as a soothing hot shower. Starting again with fresh inspiration, that's the way I feel about a good breakfast, too. This one glows with all the colors of the young morning sky, starting with a golden tofu scramble enhanced with orange shredded carrots, fading into a deep red Roma tomato at the bottom. Stacked on top of a crisply toasted English muffin, this simple sandwich allows anyone to experience that same daily rejuvenation, no matter what time the alarm clock sounds.

2 tablespoons olive oil, divided
1 small yellow onion, diced
1 clove garlic, minced
½ cup shredded carrots
1 (14-ounce) package extra-firm tofu, drained
2 tablespoons nutritional yeast
½ teaspoon black salt (kala namak)
¼ teaspoon ground turmeric
¼ teaspoon ground black pepper

To Assemble:
4 English muffins, split
2 Roma tomatoes, sliced

Preheat your oven to 400°F.

Drizzle 1 tablespoon of oil all over a half sheet pan, tilting it around to evenly coat the bottom. Add the onion, garlic, and carrots on top and place the sheet pan in the center of your oven. Bake for 10 minutes, until softened and aromatic.

Remove the sheet pan and roughly crumble the tofu on top. Sprinkle with nutritional yeast, black salt, turmeric, and pepper. Drizzle the remaining tablespoon of oil on top and stir thoroughly to combine. Return the sheet pan to the oven and bake for another 10 minutes.

Stir well and slide the scramble over to one side of the sheet pan. Place the split English muffins on the empty side of sheet, cut sides facing up. Place the sheet on the top rack of the oven and bake for a final 6 to 10 minutes, until the muffins are toasted.

To complete the sandwiches, start with a layer of sliced tomatoes on the bottom half of an English muffin, top with ¼ of the tofu scramble, and finish with the top half of the muffin. Repeat with the remaining ingredients and serve hot.

> Breakfast should be fun; don't be afraid to play with your food! Instead of regular English muffins, try using your favorite bagels, sandwich bread, or frozen waffles.

SUPER-SIZED POP ART TART

MAKES 8 TO 10 SERVINGS

Putting the "art" back into Pop-Tarts®, this giant pastry makes a mockery of the diminutive single servings. Bigger is better for the ideal ration of crust to filling, allowing you a bigger bite of gooey, jammy fruit preserves than would ever fit in an entire hand pie. Icing is essential to the experience and this bold pink lacquer does not disappoint. Tinted using only beet juice, it's an all-natural beacon on the breakfast table, enticing kids and adults alike to gather 'round. Truth be told, you could just as happily serve your artistic masterpiece as a snack or dessert, without any negative critiques.

PASTRY & FILLING:
2½ cups all-purpose flour
2 teaspoons granulated sugar
½ teaspoon salt
¾ cup vegan butter, chilled and cut
    into small pieces
1 tablespoon lemon juice
2–4 tablespoons ice-cold water
1 cup fruit preserves

PINK ICING:
2 cups confectioners' sugar
1 teaspoon vanilla extract
2–3 tablespoons beet juice
2–3 tablespoons rainbow sprinkles

> The naturally rosy hue of this icing comes entirely from beets! You can either use cold-pressed beet juice, or simply the liquid from canned beets. It's such a small amount that it won't affect the flavor.

To make the pastry, begin by placing the flour, sugar, and salt in a large bowl. Use a pastry cutter or two forks to cut in the pieces of butter. A few small chunks of butter should remain visible, but nothing larger than pea-sized. Sprinkle lemon juice and 1 tablespoon of water into the bowl and stir well with a wide spatula. Sometimes it can be difficult to get the liquids properly incorporated, so it may be helpful to get in there and mix with your hands. If the dough holds together when squeezed, you're set. If it remains crumbly, keep adding water, just a teaspoon at a time, and mix thoroughly until the dough is cohesive. Do your best not to over-mix or over-handle the dough, as this will make it tough when baked.

Divide the dough into two equal portions. Shape them into rounded rectangles and flatten them into disks about ½-inch thick. Wrap each tightly with plastic wrap and stash them in the fridge. Let chill for at least an hour, or up to a week. To save the unbaked dough even longer, store the pieces in your freezer for up to 6 months (don't forget to label them clearly!).

When you're ready to roll, preheat your oven to 350°F. Lightly dust a clean, flat surface with an even coating of flour. Work on one disk of dough at a time, and coat both sides lightly with additional flour. Starting at the center of the disk, use your rolling pin to apply light pressure while rolling outwards to the edges. Roll the dough out into a rectangle, about as wide as a half sheet pan but not quite as long. It may be helpful to periodically lift the dough to ensure that it's not adhering to the counter.

(Continued on next page)

Carefully transfer the dough to an ungreased half sheet pan and lightly prick all over with a fork. Spread the fruit preserves all over, leaving about ½-inch border around the edge clear.

Repeat the process with the second piece of dough, laying it over the jam-topped piece gently. Crimp the edges with a fork, sealing it firmly so the jam doesn't escape. Trim away any rough edges and prick the top carefully to vent.

Bake in the center of your oven for 30 to 35 minutes, or until lightly golden brown. Remove from oven and allow to cool until just barely warm.

To make the icing, simply whisk together the confectioners' sugar, vanilla, and 2 tablespoons of beet juice. Mix thoroughly until completely smooth. Add more beet juice if needed to reach a good consistency for drizzling, approximately the same thickness as pancake batter.

Pour the icing all over the baked and cooled tart, spreading it out as evenly as possible. Top with sprinkles and either let stand at room temperature for an hour to set or serve right away for a gooier experience.

TOFU SHAKSHUKA

MAKES 4 TO 5 SERVINGS

Slowly gaining recognition across the fifty united states, the word "shakshuka" is practically synonymous with breakfast in Israel. Burgeoning bowls of spicy red stew bubble up vigorously every morning, crowned with poached eggs floating amongst the tomatoes and peppers. It's a simple pleasure that is just as easily translated for vegan tastes, complete with a punch of protein to start your day off right. Pair it with lightly toasted pita bread to serve more diners, or to satisfy those with bigger appetites.

SHAKSHUKA STEW:

- 2 medium red bell peppers, diced
- 1 large red onion, diced
- 2 tablespoons olive oil
- 2 teaspoons ground cumin
- 1 teaspoon ground coriander
- 1 teaspoon smoked paprika
- ½ teaspoon crushed red pepper flakes
- ½ teaspoon salt
- 2 (14-ounce) cans fire roasted diced tomatoes
- 2 tablespoons fresh parsley, minced (optional)

POACHED TOFU:

- 1 (14-ounce) packaged firm tofu, drained
- 2 tablespoons nutritional yeast
- ½ teaspoon black salt (kala namak)

Preheat your oven to 400°F.

Place the diced peppers and onion on a half sheet pan, drizzle with the oil, and toss to coat. Set the pan in the center of the oven and bake for 10 minutes. Add the cumin, coriander, paprika, red pepper flakes, salt, and tomatoes, stirring gently to combine. Roast for another 10 to 12 minutes, until the vegetables are softened, and the stew is bubbling gently around the edges.

Meanwhile, prepare the tofu by slicing it lengthwise into thirds. Use a small round and/or fluted cookie cutter to punch out about 4 circles from each slab. Gently toss with nutritional yeast and black salt to coat.

Remove the baking sheet from the oven. Carefully press your tofu rounds into the stew at regular intervals. Roast for a final 5 to 8 minutes, until the tofu is hot all the way through.

Garnish with minced parsley, if desired, and serve piping hot.

> *If you don't care so much about the visuals and don't want to "waste" the corners, feel free to simply cut the tofu into small squares. I happen to love using the leftover tofu in scrambles, salads, and curries.*

SNACKS & APPS

CAULIFLOWER TEMPURA

MAKES 4 SERVINGS

How could something cooked in gallons of bubbling hot oil possibly emerge so light and crisp? Such is the conundrum of tempura, a perennial deep fried favorite sizzling at every Japanese eatery, near and far. The secret is a combination of panko breadcrumbs and the effervescent lift of sparkling seltzer. Working in concert, the outside coating cooks quickly and practically shatters on impact. Use this same trick in the oven to cut down on messy grease splatters and get straight to the good stuff. Cauliflower florets are ideal for this treatment, turning mere vegetables into compulsively snackable morsels. Dress them up with a spicy finishing sauce like they do in restaurants, and you'll have a healthy party-starter at home in an instant.

CAULIFLOWER TEMPURA:
2 tablespoons olive oil, divided
1 head cauliflower (about 4 cups
    florets)
½ cup all-purpose flour
½ teaspoon baking soda
½ teaspoon salt
½ teaspoon ground black pepper
½ cup seltzer or soda water
1 cup panko breadcrumbs

DYNAMITE SAUCE:
½ cup plain, unsweetened vegan
    yogurt
1 teaspoon granulated sugar
1–3 teaspoons chili sauce or sriracha

Preheat your oven to 400°F and grease a half sheet pan with 1 tablespoon of the oil.

Cut the cauliflower into florets and discard or reserve the core for another use (you can "rice" it in the food processor and freeze it for later!).

In a medium bowl, whisk together the flour, baking soda, salt, and pepper. Slowly pour in the seltzer or soda water to prevent it from bubbling over, and whisk until smooth. Place the panko in a separate bowl and prepare to start the breading.

Toss a few florets into the bowl of batter at a time, using a fork to turn them over and fully coat all sides. Tap off any excess before transferring them to the bowl of panko. Toss to coat, and transfer to the prepared sheet pan. Repeat this process until all the cauliflower is fully breaded. Make sure the pieces are in a single layer, without overlapping, with at least a little bit of space in between for even cooking.

Drizzle with the remaining oil and bake for 15 minutes, until fork-tender and beautifully burnished brown.

While the cauliflower is baking, whip up the dynamite sauce by simply mixing the yogurt and sugar, adding hot sauce to taste.

Serve while the cauliflower is still piping hot and perfectly crisp.

DILL PICKLE CHICKPEA CRUNCHIES

MAKES 1½ TO 2 CUPS; 3 TO 4 SERVINGS

Cooked chickpeas are soaked in a classic pickle brine overnight before being slowly roasted to crunchy perfection. A full battery of herbs and spices join the mix, creating a balanced flavor profile that's far more satisfying than your average salty snack. Full of good stuff like fiber and protein, a handful will happily keep hunger at bay, and help you resist the urge to plunge into the pickle jar for a straight shot of sodium.

BRINE AND BEANS:

½ cup cold water

½ cup white vinegar

¼ cup apple cider vinegar

1 tablespoon granulated sugar or
    light agave nectar

2 (14-ounce) cans (3 cups cooked)
    chickpeas, drained

SEASONINGS:

2 tablespoons olive oil

¼ cup roughly chopped fresh dill

3 cloves garlic, finely minced

1 teaspoon coarse sea salt or kosher
    salt

½ teaspoon dry mustard powder

¼ teaspoon ground coriander

¼ teaspoon celery seed

⅛ teaspoon ground black pepper

⅛ teaspoon red pepper flakes

Place all the ingredients for the brine in a medium-sized glass jar, including the chickpeas, shake it vigorously to combine, and place it in the fridge. Allow the brine to infuse into the beans for 12 to 24 hours. The longer the chickpeas soak, the more strongly they'll be flavored, so try them after 12 hours and continue soaking according to your flavor preference. Bear in mind that the bite will mellow significantly after baking, so don't be afraid of having very vinegary beans at this stage.

Once the chickpeas have been "pickled," drain them thoroughly but do not rinse. Preheat your oven to 375°F while you measure out and prep the seasonings. Toss the chickpeas into a bowl along with the oil and all the aromatics, stirring so that every last bean is thoroughly coated. Transfer to a half sheet pan or jellyroll pan lined with aluminum foil or parchment paper, spreading them out into one even layer.

Bake for 45 to 60 minutes, stirring every 15 minutes or so, until the chickpeas have shrunk in size and are golden-brown, with darker spots in some areas. It can be hard to tell when they're done since the chickpeas will continue to crisp up as they cool, but listen closely and they should rattle when you shake the pan. Remove from heat and let cool completely before snacking and/or storing in an airtight container.

Stashed away in a dry, cool place, the chickpea crunchies will keep for about 1 week.

FALAFEL PANISSE WITH WHIPPED TAHINI

MAKES ABOUT 40 TO 45 PANISSE AND 1 CUP WHIPPED TAHINI; 4 TO 5 SERVINGS

Falling somewhere between French fries and seared polenta, these chickpea-based batons are taking the world by storm. Smooth, almost custard-like interiors are concealed by immaculately crisp crusts. Seasoned simply with coarse salt, they're a simple pleasure to pair with a round of drinks, but when spiced up to match the flavor of herbaceous falafel, they shine with even greater vibrancy. Cumin and coriander dance amidst flurries of green parsley and cilantro, taking the humble snack to all new heights. Light, fluffy whipped tahini brings each bite back down to earth gently, landing gracefully with resounding nutty, earthy flavor. It's so hard to stop at one small portion, I wouldn't blame you for turning this quick fix into a full meal.

FALAFEL PANISSE:

2 cups chickpea flour
1 tablespoon ground cumin
2½ teaspoons ground coriander
1½ teaspoons garlic powder
1 teaspoon smoked paprika
¾ teaspoon salt
3½ cups vegetable stock
3 tablespoons olive oil, divided
1 cup fresh parsley, minced
½ cup fresh cilantro, minced

WHIPPED TAHINI:

½ cup tahini
1 tablespoon fresh parsley, finely minced
1 teaspoon garlic powder
¼ teaspoon salt
2 tablespoons lemon juice
⅓ cup water

Preheat your oven to 350°F. Lightly grease a quarter sheet pan and set aside.

In a large bowl, whisk together the chickpea flour, cumin, coriander, garlic powder, paprika, and salt. Slowly pour in the vegetable stock, along with 1 tablespoon of the oil, while stirring constantly. The mixture will soon become too thick to whisk, so switch to a spatula to make sure everything is incorporated. Add the minced parsley and cilantro, mixing thoroughly until the herbs are evenly distributed throughout the batter.

Smooth the mixture into your prepared sheet pan, using your spatula to massage it into as even a layer as possible. This is critical for even cooking, so take your time to get it right.

Bake for 20 minutes, until set and lightly crackled on top. Let cool before placing the sheet in your fridge to chill.

Meanwhile, prepare the whipped tahini. Place the tahini in a medium bowl along with the parsley, garlic, salt, and lemon juice. Stir to combine. Switch to a whisk and slowly drizzle in the water, whisking constantly, until fully incorporated. The mixture should be light, creamy, and almost fluffy in consistency, like partially melted frosting. Chill until ready to serve.

(Continued on next page)

Once the panisse mixture has cooled and solidified, turn it out onto a cutting board and slice it into fingers about ¾-inch × 3 inches. No need to break out the ruler; as long as they're consistent, the exact measurements aren't critical!

Turn up the oven temperature to 425°F.

Place the pieces on a half sheet pan lined with parchment paper or a silicone baking mat, spaced about ¼-inch apart, and brush with 1 tablespoon of the remaining oil. Bake for 15 minutes, until lightly browned around the edges.

Flip and brush with the final tablespoon of oil. Bake for an additional 10 to 15 minutes, until browned and crispy all over.

Serve hot alongside cool whipped tahini.

FURIKAKE AVOCADO FRIES

MAKES 4 SERVINGS

"FryDay" celebrations used to be a weekly affair, but all that extra grease started adding up on my kitchen walls and waistline. Seeking a healthier way to get my French fry fix, I turned to my trusty oven. Furikake, rather than a heavy batter, coats thick planks of ripe avocado for a satisfying change of pace. These fries rely entirely on the natural fats of the avocado, without any added oil. Crispy on the outside, they're covered in nutty toasted sesame seeds and satisfyingly salty nori crisps, yet lusciously creamy on the inside. If you simply must have a dip, try mixing vegan mayo and sriracha to taste for a spicy aioli on the side, but honestly, it feels superfluous for such a perfect food.

FURIKAKE:
2 sheets toasted nori
¼ cup hemp seeds
2 tablespoons sesame seeds
2 tablespoons nutritional yeast
1 tablespoon dried parsley
¼ teaspoon garlic powder
¼ teaspoon salt

AVOCADO FRIES:
3 tablespoons water
1 tablespoon ground flaxseeds
2 small avocados
2 tablespoons rice vinegar
¼ cup tapioca starch

> Luscious, buttery green orbs of savory delight, avocados can be as heavenly as they are torturous. The key to success is in proper avocado management. Notoriously fickle, they'll remain rock-hard for a week, impenetrable and unyielding. The window of perfection, soft and creamy yet still sliceable, closes quickly. For the best bite, you want to use fully ripe but still firm fruits here. If it seems like they could maybe use just one more day to serve on a salad, that's just the ticket.

To make the furikake, roughly crumble the toasted nori into a medium bowl. Use a spice grinder if you'd like a finely, more consistent texture, or simply rub it between your fingers until you have satisfactory flakes. Add the hemp seeds, sesame seeds, nutritional yeast, dried parsley, garlic powder, and salt. Stir well to combine.

If not using immediately, store in an airtight container in a dry, cool place for up to 3 weeks.

Moving on to the avocado fries, preheat your oven to 450°F. Line a half sheet pan with parchment paper or a silicone baking mat and set aside.

Whisk together the water and flaxseeds in a medium bowl and let sit for 15 minutes to thicken. Meanwhile, pit, peel, and cut the avocados into thin wedges, tossing them gently with vinegar to prevent them from browning.

Place the avocado pieces in a small bowl with the starch, tossing gently to coat. Shake off any excess starch before placing them in the flax mixture, just a few pieces at a time. Make sure they're coated before finally tossing the pieces with furikake. Press lightly to make sure it adheres, covering the entire exterior.

Transfer the avocado wedges to your prepared sheet pan, repeating as necessary until all the pieces are coated. Bake for 12 to 15 minutes, or until crisp and golden brown all over.

Serve hot, with vegan mayonnaise or dynamite sauce (page 31) if desired.

GREENS AND BEANS CROSTINI

MAKES 8 SERVINGS

Lightly toasted slices of fresh bread are the perfect vehicle for a wide range of toppings, limited only by what you have in the fridge and pantry. For a simple and healthy appetizer, my go-to combination always involves some sort of green vegetable and beans. In this combination, the sharp bitterness of broccoli rabe is kept at bay with zesty, subtly sweet notes of orange punctuating a base of white bean puree. For a milder leafy base, try roasting tender baby bok choy instead. Paired with creamy white beans and umami-rich sundried tomatoes, it's a party-starter that will make your taste buds get up and dance.

1 bunch (1 pound) broccoli rabe, trimmed and roughly chopped
¼ cup olive oil, divided
1 teaspoon salt, divided
1 (15-ounce) can (or 1½ cups cooked) white beans, drained and rinsed
1 clove garlic, finely minced
1 teaspoon orange zest
⅛ teaspoon ground black pepper
8 slices sourdough or French bread, sliced ½-inch thick
½ cup sundried tomatoes, julienned
1 scallion, thinly sliced

Preheat your oven to 400°F and line two half sheet pans with parchment paper or silicone baking mats. Toss the broccoli rabe with 2 tablespoons of oil and ½ teaspoon of salt. Distribute equally between the two sheets, spreading them out in the middle of each one. Make sure there's very little overlap to prevent them from simply steaming. Roast for 8 minutes, until bright green.

Meanwhile, place the beans, garlic, orange zest, pepper, and remaining salt in a medium bowl. Mash vigorously with a sturdy fork or more preferably, with a potato masher, until the beans are broken down and creamy, but not perfectly smooth—you want to leave a bit of texture here.

Coat the bread with the remaining oil and arrange the slices around the edges of the sheet pans. Continue to roast until the broccoli rabe is gently caramelized around the edges and the bread is lightly toasted; about 7 to 9 minutes longer.

Spread the mashed bean mixture on top of the toast. Mound the broccoli rabe on top, and finish with the sundried tomatoes and scallion.

HOT SMASHED HUMMUS

MAKES 10 TO 12 SERVINGS

Hummus makes the world go 'round. Everyone wants to claim it as their own, in Greece, Israel, Egypt, and beyond. One thing we can all agree on, however, is that hummus is 100 percent delicious, no matter where it came from. Much ado has been made about achieving the silkiest, smoothest, creamiest blend possible, going so far as to painstakingly peel each individual chickpea by hand, but I'm here to say that it might be even more sensational taken in exactly the opposite direction. A rustic riot of texture, warm chickpeas that are crushed with a potato masher have much more character than some anonymous, homogenous paste. There's truly no wrong way to make hummus, so why not try roughing it this time?

1 head garlic (8–10 cloves)
½ cup olive oil, divided
2 (15-ounce) cans (3 cups cooked) chickpeas
¼ cup tahini
¼ cup lemon juice
½ teaspoon smoked paprika
½ teaspoon ground cumin
½ teaspoon salt

If you're a smooth criminal that demands flawlessly creamy, unblemished bowls of hummus, feel free to pull out your food processor and blend the mixture instead. Be sure to scrape down the sides of the canister to make sure it's all incorporated into a silken puree.

Preheat your oven to 350°F and slice the very top off the garlic, exposing the ends of the cloves within. Drizzle with 1 tablespoon of the olive oil and wrap in aluminum foil. Set aside.

Drain the chickpeas but reserve the aquafaba. Toss the beans with 2 tablespoons of the oil and spread them out evenly on a sheet pan lined with parchment paper or a silicone baking sheet. Leave a little space at the end of the pan clear, where you can place the wrapped head of garlic.

Bake for 35 to 45 minutes, until the chickpeas are firm, and the garlic is soft. Let rest until the garlic is cool enough to handle and squeeze the cloves out into a medium bowl. Measure out about ½ cup of the chickpeas and set them aside. Add the rest to the bowl, along with another ¼ cup of oil, the tahini, lemon juice, paprika, cumin, and salt. Use a potato masher to go to town! Mash and smash the mixture until the beans and garlic are broken down and creamy. Slowly drizzle in aquafaba, 1 tablespoon at a time, until it reaches your desired consistency. You won't need all of it; save the leftover aquafaba in an airtight container in the fridge for another recipe (like meringues!).

Transfer the hummus to a serving dish and top with the last remaining tablespoon of oil and the reserved, whole chickpeas. Dig in while still warm.

MUSHROOM LARB

MAKES 3 TO 4 SERVINGS

The beauty of larb, otherwise written as laab, lahb, larp, laap, or lahp, and prepared just as many ways, is that it comes together in a flash. Brilliantly perfumed with a bouquet of fresh herbs and spices, this stunningly simple yet impossibly complex dish is a revelation in every bite. Offering a fresh experience with every mouthful, opportunities for different variations with every passing season abound. Over the years, I've enjoyed many riffs on this timeless theme, often with the unmistakable umami of chopped mushrooms sprinkled throughout. Even in the heat of summer, the quietly smoldering flavor is a welcome escape, tempered by the cooling foil of crisp lettuce cups for serving. It's well worth that fleeting moment in the fire.

MUSHROOM LARB:

2 tablespoons peanut oil, divided
1 pound cremini or button
    mushrooms, roughly chopped
3 cloves garlic, minced
1 tablespoon minced fresh ginger
⅓ cup minced shallot or yellow onion
1 (12-ounce) package tempeh,
    crumbled
2 tablespoons lime juice
2 tablespoons soy sauce
1 teaspoon sesame oil
1 tablespoon coconut sugar or light
    brown sugar, firmly packed
½–1 teaspoon crushed red pepper
    flakes, divided
2 scallions, thinly sliced
2 tablespoons roughly chopped fresh
    mint

TO SERVE:

1 head romaine, savoy cabbage, or
    butter lettuce, leaves separated
¼ cup roasted peanuts, roughly
    chopped

Preheat your oven to 400°F and drizzle a half sheet pan with 1 tablespoon of the peanut oil.

Spread the chopped mushrooms out in the center of the sheet pan, leaving the borders clear. Sprinkle the garlic, ginger, and shallot or onion on top, distributing it as evenly as possible. Crumble the tempeh around the edges, allowing it full contact with the metal pan.

Drizzle everything with the remaining peanut oil, lime juice, soy sauce, and sesame oil. Sprinkle the sugar and ½ teaspoon red pepper flakes right on top, without stirring.

Slide the whole sheet into the oven and roast for 20 minutes, stirring halfway through.

Once the tempeh is golden brown and the mushrooms have wilted considerably, remove the mixture from the oven and let cool for 5 minutes. Fold in the scallions and mint and incorporate more red pepper flakes if desired. Season to taste.

Transfer to a serving dish alongside lettuce or cabbage leaves and chopped peanuts. Let guests assemble their own wraps, loading up the meaty mushrooms and nuts to their hearts' content.

NACHO MAMMA LOADED TORTILLA CHIPS

MAKES 5 TO 6 SERVINGS

In the same spirit of equally amorphous concepts like salads and curries, basically anything you throw on top of tortilla chips can be considered nachos. There's no one "right" or "best" way to make nachos; they're the ultimate blank slate, infinitely adaptable to your personal tastes. Personally, I must insist that some form of cheese or queso is mandatory, but that doesn't mean processed vegan shreds or prepared queso is the only way. Whip up a super-fast cheesy tahini sauce to make this instant party-starter in a flash. Load up on all the toppings to make every bite a fiesta in your mouth. Your Mexican mama might not have made it this way, but if she would give it a try, I have a feeling she would approve.

TAHINI NACHO SAUCE:

½ cup tahini
½ cup plain, unsweetened non-dairy milk
⅓ cup nutritional yeast
¼ cup olive oil
2 tablespoons lime juice
2 tablespoons rice vinegar
2 tablespoons water
½ teaspoon ground cumin
½ teaspoon smoked paprika
½ teaspoon garlic powder
½ teaspoon chili powder
¼ teaspoon ground turmeric
½ teaspoon salt

TO ASSEMBLE:

1 (10–12 ounce) bag tortilla chips
1 (14-ounce) can black beans, drained and rinsed
2 tomatoes or 1 cup cherry tomatoes, diced
1–2 medium avocados, sliced or diced
¼ red onion, finely diced
1–2 jalapeños, thinly sliced
¼ cup fresh cilantro, minced

OPTIONAL ADDITIONS:

Corn kernels
Sliced radishes
Thinly sliced scallions
Hot sauce
Sliced olives
Refried beans
Pepitas (hulled pumpkin seeds)
Shredded cabbage
Chopped bell peppers

To begin, preheat your oven to 350°F.

The sauce is really the only component you need to prepare, and you can make it well in advance, ready to go whenever cravings strike. First, stir the tahini thoroughly to blend together all the oils and solids, since it's apt to separate over time.

Place the smooth tahini in a large bowl and whisk in the non-dairy milk, nutritional yeast, olive oil, lime juice, and vinegar. At first, it will be difficult to stir and look a bit curdled, but have no fear. Keep on whisking until the mixture smooths out, and add in the water to slightly thin. Introduce the spices and seasonings last, whisking to incorporate.

Spread the tortilla chips out in an even layer on a half sheet pan, allowing only a little bit of overlap. You want as much as of the chips exposed as possible for more complete coverage. Place the sheet in the oven for 8 to 10 minutes, to re-crisp and warm the chips through.

Remove the sheet from the oven and drizzle generously with about half of the nacho sauce. You should have plenty left over for topping, dipping, or saving for later. Evenly sprinkle the beans and tomatoes on top before baking for an additional 5 minutes, to slightly thicken the sauce and tenderize the tomatoes.

Top with avocado, red onion, jalapeños, fresh cilantro, and any of the other optional additions, as desired.

Serve hot, right off the sheet pan, to an adoring crowd.

OATSOME ENERGY BARS

MAKES 20 TO 24 BARS

Oats: They're not just for breakfast anymore! For a grab-and-go snack, nothing beats the slow-burning energy of these whole rolled grains. They won't melt in the sun, crumble in transit, or send you spinning on a sugar high. Swap in any of your favorite dried fruits and nuts to choose your own flavorful adventure.

2 cups old-fashioned rolled oats
2 cups puffed millet or brown rice
 cereal
½ cup whole wheat flour
½ cup unsweetened coconut flakes
½ cup raw almonds
¼ cup raisins
¼ cup roughly chopped raw walnuts
¼ cup pepitas (hulled pumpkin seeds)
¼ cup ground flaxseeds
¼ cup chia seeds
1 teaspoon ground cinnamon
½ teaspoon salt
1 cup unsweetened applesauce
⅔ cup coconut sugar or dark brown
 sugar, firmly packed

Preheat your oven to 325°F and line a quarter sheet pan with foil. Lightly grease and set aside.

In a large bowl, combine the oats, puffed millet or brown rice cereal, whole wheat flour, coconut flakes, almonds, raisins, walnuts, pepitas, ground flaxseeds, chia seeds, cinnamon, and salt. Stir thoroughly to make sure all the ingredients are evenly distributed throughout the mixture.

In a separate bowl, combine the applesauce and sugar. Once smooth, add the wet ingredients to the bowl of dry, stirring with a wide spatula to coat. Make sure all the dry goods are moistened and slightly sticky.

Transfer the mixture to your prepared sheet pan, pressing firmly into an even layer with lightly moistened hands.

Bake in the center of your oven for 24 to 28 minutes, rotating about halfway through. The bars should be lightly golden brown around the edges when finished.

Let cool completely, and chill for about an hour for the cleanest cuts. Use the foil overhanging the edges like a sling to pull the full sheet of bars out and onto a cutting board. Slice into squares and enjoy!

For long term storage, wrap individually in plastic or pop into little zip-top bags. Stash them in the fridge for up to a week, or in the freezer for 2 to 3 months.

OKONOMIYAKI

MAKES 6 TO 8 SERVINGS

Anything goes with okonomiyaki! It literally means "as you like it," incorporating any number of savory additions according to the individual eater's tastes. Essentially a large pancake, it's a very popular type of street food hailing from Osaka, Japan. Regional differences mandate particular inclusions, but there are truly no wrong answers here. Shredded cabbage is really the only mandatory ingredient, with other options ranging from mushrooms, bean sprouts, konjac, mochi, cheese, and even noodles. Don't be afraid to experiment!

OKONOMIYAKI:
2 teaspoons toasted sesame oil
1½ cups chickpea flour
1¾ teaspoons baking powder
½ teaspoon salt
1½ cups water
2 tablespoons soy sauce
1 pound (about 10 cups) coleslaw mix
    or shredded cabbage
6 scallions, sliced in ½-inch lengths
1 tablespoon pickled ginger (beni
    shōga), minced

OKONOMIYAKI SAUCE:
3 tablespoons tomato sauce
1 tablespoons soy sauce
2 teaspoons maple syrup

TO SERVE:
¼ cup vegan mayonnaise
Shredded nori, to taste

Preheat your oven to 400°F degrees and set out a half sheet pan. Drizzle the sesame oil evenly across the bottom and set aside.

In a large bowl, whisk together the chickpea flour, baking powder, and salt. Once thoroughly blended, whisk in the water and soy sauce, stirring vigorously until smooth. Make sure there are no lumps remaining.

Scatter the coleslaw or cabbage evenly over the greased sheet pan, along with the scallion and ginger. Gently pour the chickpea flour batter on top, being careful not to disturb the vegetables. Tap the pan lightly on the counter to release any air bubbles.

Bake for 15 to 20 minutes until very lightly browned around the edges and the cabbage is tender.

While the pancake itself is baking, prepare the sauce by whisking together the tomato sauce, soy sauce, and maple syrup until smooth.

To serve, cut the pancake into rectangles and drizzle with the okonomiyaki sauce and mayonnaise as desired. Top with a pinch of shredded nori and eat right away, while piping hot.

> For a spicier bite, try replacing 1 to 2 cups of the plain cabbage with kimchi.

PRETZEL FOCACCIA

MAKES 20 TO 24 SERVINGS

Dark and mysterious, the deeply burnished crust lets you know at a glance that it's not just your average slab of flatbread. Brushing the surface of the dough with a baking soda and water mixture alkalizes the exterior, producing a richly caramelized, mahogany brown crust, just like a properly boiled and baked soft pretzel. Imparting a signature slightly bitter twang, it's best served with tangy whole stoneground mustard.

3½ cups warm water, divided
1 tablespoon granulated sugar
1 (¼-ounce) packet (2¼ teaspoons) active dry yeast
6½ cups all-purpose flour
1½ teaspoons salt
2 tablespoons olive oil, divided
¼ cup aquafaba
1½ tablespoons baking soda
2 tablespoons vegan butter, melted
½ teaspoon coarse or flaky salt

Store leftovers in an airtight container at room temperature for up to 3 days. Alternately, to freeze, wrap individual portions in plastic wrap, stack in an airtight container, and freeze for up to 3 months. To reheat the focaccia, remove the plastic wrap and lay the pieces out on an ungreased sheet pan. Reheat in a 350°F oven for 10 minutes, or until warm all the way through.

In a large bowl, mix together ½ cup of the warm water, sugar, and yeast. Allow 10 to 15 minutes for the yeast to reactivate, becoming foamy and aromatic. Add 2 more cups of water along with half of the flour. Stir vigorously with a sturdy spoon or spatula until incorporated. Introduce the remaining water and flour, mixing well. Continue to stir aggressively for 5 to 8 minutes to beat out any remaining lumps. The mixture should be very loose and sticky, much more like cake batter than typical bread dough.

Coat a second large bowl with 1 tablespoon of oil. Transfer the soupy mix to the greased bowl, cover, and stash in the fridge overnight. Give it at least 12 hours, and up to 3 days, to develop the best flavor.

When you're ready to bake, thoroughly coat a half sheet pan with 1 tablespoon oil, making sure every corner and side is fully covered. Scrape the dough out onto your sheet pan and use your hands to gently press it out to evenly fill to space. You may want to lightly grease your hands if the mixture is unmanageably sticky.

Let rest at room temperature for 30 to 45 minutes, until doubled in volume. Begin preheating your oven to 450°F during the final 15 minutes of rising.

Meanwhile, whisk together the aquafaba and baking soda, mixing very well, to completely dissolve and incorporate the powder. Gently brush the mixture over the raw dough using a pastry brush, making sure to coat the surface evenly. Any pockets of unmixed baking soda will be unpleasantly bitter.

Bake in your preheated oven for 18 to 20 minutes, until darkly burnished to a mahogany finish. While still hot, brush with melted vegan butter and sprinkle all over with coarse or flaky salt. Let cool for at least 15 to 20 minutes before slicing into rectangles or squares, as desired. Enjoy warm or at room temperature.

PUPPY TRAINING TREATS

MAKES 200 TO 225 TINY TREATS

Puppy guidebooks very kindly described my new baby as a breed with "a casual attitude towards obedience." After three years of slow, almost imperceptible progress, I can't say they were wrong. That means that training is a constant project for us both, though I think he might be enjoying it more than I am. What's not to like about an activity that involves lots of treats, after all? I started making my own little bite-sized morsels so we would never run out or pay a premium for essentially doggie junk food. The formula is extremely flexible based on what you have on hand, which also means you can make new and exciting flavors to keep pickier eaters entertained. My guy? Well, admittedly he would eat a used Band-Aid, so he might not be the most discerning critic, but he gives it two paws up (hopefully not on the sofa)!

1½ cups rolled oats
½ cup pumpkin puree, mashed
    bananas, or unsweetened
    applesauce
¼ cup creamy peanut butter, almond
    butter, cashew butter, or tahini
2 tablespoons ground flaxseeds or
    chia seeds
3–5 tablespoons water

Preheat the oven to 350°F and line a half sheet pan with parchment paper.

Place the oats in your blender and pulse until they're broken down into a fine flour. Add the puree or mash of your choice along with the nut butter and ground seeds. Blend on high speed until smooth, slowly drizzling in enough water to keep everything incorporated. It will be a thick, sticky mixture.

Transfer the dough to your prepared baking sheet and use a nonstick spatula to smooth it out in an even layer, about ¼-inch thick.

Bake in the center of your oven for 10 minutes. Carefully remove the sheet from the oven and use a pizza cutter to score the treats into ¼-inch squares. Return the pan to the oven and bake for another 20 to 25 minutes, until lightly browned and dry to the touch.

Allow to cool completely before breaking all the pieces apart. Store in an airtight container in the fridge for up to 2 weeks, or in the freezer for up to 6 months.

SOUR CREAM AND ONION ZUCCHINI CHIPS

MAKES 2 TO 4 SERVINGS

America's favorite potato chip seasoning can spice up far more than just spuds. These crisp rounds are baked rather than fried, which makes them smart snacks, both low-fat and low-calorie. It's no struggle convincing picky eaters to make room for their veggies when these tangy, savory flavors beckon. Shockingly simple to whip up, the hardest part of the recipe is waiting while they bake low and slow for the perfect crunchy texture all the way through.

1 pound (1 very large or 2 medium-large) zucchini
1 tablespoon apple cider vinegar
2 teaspoons olive oil
1 tablespoon onion powder
1 tablespoon nutritional yeast
2 teaspoons dried chives
1 teaspoon garlic powder
1 teaspoon dried parsley
½ teaspoon salt

Preheat your oven to 275°F and line two half sheet pans with silicon baking mats or parchment paper. Set aside.

Use a mandoline or very sharp knife to cut the zucchini into 1mm-thick slices, keeping them as consistent as possible. This will allow them to cook more evenly, ensuring crispness throughout.

Place in a large bowl and toss with all the remaining ingredients, distributing the spices and coating the pieces well.

Place the zucchini on your prepared sheet pans, spreading them out so that none overlap.

Bake for 1 to 1¼ hours, rotating the sheets every 15 minutes, until golden brown and dry to the touch.

Let cool completely before serving or storing in an airtight container for up to 3 days. They may lose crispness over time but will still taste just as good.

SUPER CORNY QUESADILLA

Literally meaning "little cheesy thing," the original quesadillas were essentially savory hand pies using tortillas instead of pastry. A viral hit since their invention in the early sixteenth century, their universal appeal of this Mexican staple owes to the simplicity of the concept, perfect for feeding one or one hundred. When it's more like the latter, don't waste time with small skillets; this is a job for the sheet pan! Create cheesy snacks en masse by overlapping soft flour tortillas, baking them to golden, crispy finish, and cutting it into hearty wedges for the hungry hordes. Mashed white beans do double duty as an uncanny cheesy sauce and substantive legume filling. Pair that with tender, naturally sweet corn kernels and hot jalapeños, and you'll have a whole different kind of sharable sensation at hand.

CHEESY REFRIED WHITE BEANS:

1 (14-ounce) can (1½ cups cooked)
   white beans, drained
⅓ cup nutritional yeast
3 tablespoons olive oil
1 tablespoon apple cider vinegar
1 teaspoon onion powder
½ teaspoon smoked paprika
½ teaspoon garlic powder
¼ teaspoon chili powder
½ teaspoon salt

TO ASSEMBLE:

8–10 large (9- or 10-inch) flour tortillas
1½ cups corn kernels, fresh, canned
   and drained, or frozen and thawed
1 jalapeño, seeded and diced
2 scallions, thinly sliced
¼ cup fresh cilantro, minced

Preheat your oven to 400°F.

Place the white beans in a large bowl along with the nutritional yeast. Use a potato masher to thoroughly mash, until mostly smooth. It's fine to leave the mixture slightly chunky if you prefer the texture, too. Stir in the oil, vinegar, onion powder, paprika, garlic powder, chili powder, and salt. Once thoroughly blended and homogenous, set aside.

On a half sheet pan, place 6 tortillas around the edges so that about half of each tortilla overhangs over edge. Arrange another tortilla or two, as needed, in the center to cover the bottom of the pan completely.

Spread the cheesy seasoned beans all over, and then evenly sprinkle the corn, jalapeño, scallions, and cilantro on top.

Fold the tortilla over the filling, and place one or two in the center for complete coverage. Place a second half sheet pan on top, to keep the tortillas in place. Bake for 20 minutes, until the edges begin to brown. Remove top sheet pan and continue baking until tortillas are golden all over and perfectly crisp; about 10 to 15 minutes more.

Slice into rectangles and serve warm, with vegan sour cream and salsa, if desired.

SALADS

ALL-KALE CAESAR

MAKES 3 TO 4 SERVINGS

A light starter, bright with sharp acidity, tempered by the cooling, creamy foil of Parmesan-flecked dressing and hearty croutons, the classic Caesar salad is a foolproof start to any meal. Transform it into a truly memorable first course by replacing the token leafy greens with freshly toasted kale chips that seem to shatter upon impact. Thicker pieces tenderize to a supple, almost meaty texture. The effect is akin to swapping out watery lettuce for freshly fried potato chips; even salad-haters will come to crave it like junk food. Good thing that's a healthy addiction!

3 ounces (about 3 slices) sourdough or
    country-style bread
6 tablespoons olive oil, divided
½ teaspoon garlic powder
½ teaspoon salt, divided
1 bunch (7–8 ounces) curly kale
1 tablespoon white or chickpea miso
    paste
1 tablespoon Dijon mustard
1 teaspoon soy sauce
¼ cup nutritional yeast
¼ cup lemon juice
½ teaspoon ground black pepper

Preheat your oven to 400°F.

Prepare the croutons first by slicing the bread into 1-inch cubes. Place the pieces in a medium bowl and toss with 1 tablespoon of olive oil, along with the garlic powder and ¼ teaspoon of salt. Mix well to thoroughly coat all the bread. Transfer to a quarter sheet pan and bake for 10 to 12 minutes, stirring halfway through, until beautifully golden-brown and crisp all the way through. Set aside and reduce the oven temperature to 375°F.

Remove the stems from the kale and roughly chop or tear the leaves. Drizzle with 1 tablespoon of olive oil and sprinkle with ¼ teaspoon salt. Spread into a single layer on a half sheet pan.

Bake for 8 to 10 minutes, until the edges are shatteringly crisp, caramelized, and the inner leaves are bright green and tender. Let cool to room temperature.

Meanwhile, whip up the dressing by whisking together the miso paste, mustard, soy sauce, nutritional yeast, lemon juice, and pepper in a small bowl. Slowly stream in the remaining ¼ cup of oil to emulsify, beating vigorously until smooth and creamy.

When ready to serve, place the kale in a large bowl and toss with the croutons and dressing, mixing gently to coat and combine. Serve family-style on one large platter, or individually on smaller plates.

ALOHA RAMEN SLAW

MAKES 6 TO 8 SERVINGS

Who says salads must be austere, dietetic fare? Liven up your bowl with the color and crunch of this tropical combination! Dry ramen noodles replace standard croutons in this hot slaw, tossed in a zesty dressing that tastes like a bite of sunshine. This vibrant blend is your ticket to an island escape any day of the week.

RAMEN SLAW:

2 (3-ounce) packages ramen noodles
½ cup macadamia nuts, roughly chopped
¼ cup unsweetened coconut flakes
2 tablespoons sesame seeds
12 ounces shredded green and/or red cabbage
1 cup shelled edamame
½ cup shredded carrots
1 cup diced mango
1 medium avocado, diced
4 scallions, thinly sliced

CITRUS-SESAME DRESSING:

2 tablespoons orange juice
2 tablespoons rice vinegar
2 tablespoons olive oil
1 tablespoon toasted sesame oil
1 tablespoon soy sauce

Preheat your oven to 400°F and line a half sheet pan with parchment paper or a silicone baking mat.

Remove the seasoning packets from the ramen packages and discard or save for another use. Roughly smash or crumble the ramen blocks into bite-sized pieces and spread them in a single layer on the baking sheet. Sprinkle the macadamia nuts and coconut on top, tossing to distribute. Bake for 6 to 8 minutes until very lightly toasted, add the sesame seeds, then bake for an additional minute or two, until fragrant and golden. Watch closely so that the mixture does not burn.

While the sheet pan is still hot, add the cabbage, edamame, and carrots right on top. Toss carefully to incorporate all the crunchy goodies, while lightly warming the vegetable additions. Sprinkle the mango, avocado, and scallion on top, and set aside.

In a small bowl, vigorously whisk together the orange juice, rice vinegar, olive and sesame oil, and soy sauce. Drizzle the dressing all over the slaw mixture, tossing to coat. Transfer to a large bowl and serve right away.

You can refrigerate the finished slaw for up to 3 hours and serve chilled, but the ramen won't be quite as crisp. For the best experience, plan ahead and keep the toasted noodles, nuts, and seeds separate from the other components until you're ready to serve. Mix everything together at the last minute to enjoy the combination of both cool and crisp.

BLISTERED GREEN BEAN NIÇOISE SALAD

MAKES 4 TO 6 SERVINGS

Borrowing from the Chinese technique of wok-seared green beans, charred over high heat to retain a crisp bright green interior, French tradition is turned on its head for this unconventional arranged salad. While we're at it, let's go fish for some different oceanic flavor, like briny capers and olives, paired with the juicy layers of artichoke heart that imitate the flaky flesh of top-notch fillets. Tofu plays a convincing stand in for eggs, tasting and looking for all the world like coarsely chopped gribiche. It's not just another veganized Niçoise, but a genuine upgrade over the original.

ROASTED VEGETABLES AND DRESSING:
½ cup olive oil, divided
½ pound red-skinned baby potatoes, sliced ¼-inch thick
1 teaspoon salt, divided
½ teaspoon ground black pepper
½ pound green beans, trimmed
¼ cup red wine vinegar
½ shallot, minced (about 2 tablespoons)
2 tablespoons Dijon mustard
1 tablespoon fresh or 1 teaspoon dried thyme
1 teaspoon dried tarragon or marjoram

HARD BOILED TOFU:
¼ pound super-firm tofu, drained and cut into ¼-inch cubes
1 teaspoon chickpea miso paste
¼ teaspoon black salt (kala namak)
⅛ teaspoon turmeric

TO ASSEMBLE:
1 head Boston, bibb, or butter lettuce
1 pint cherry or grape tomatoes, halved
1 cup quartered artichoke hearts
½ cup olives
2 tablespoons capers

Preheat your oven to 400°F and install the top rack at the highest position, as close to the broiler as possible. Place the potatoes on a half sheet pan, drizzle with 1 tablespoon of olive oil, ½ teaspoon salt and ½ teaspoon pepper, and toss to coat. Arrange the potatoes so the cut sides are facing down and roast for 15 minutes.

Increase the oven temperature to 450°F and add the green beans to the sheet pan with the potatoes, along with another tablespoon of olive oil. Using tongs, toss well to combine. Roast, stirring once halfway through, until beans are tender and charred in spots; about 12 to 15 minutes. Let cool.

Meanwhile, make the dressing by combining the vinegar, shallot, mustard, thyme, tarragon, and remaining ½ teaspoon salt. Slowly drizzle in the remaining olive oil while whisking. Set aside.

In a separate bowl, toss together the tofu, miso, black salt, and turmeric until the cubes are evenly coated. This could be done up to a week in advance, stored in an airtight container in the fridge.

To assemble the salad, combine the greens with about ¼ cup of the dressing in a large bowl, tossing gently to coat. Transfer to a large platter, spreading them out nearly to the edge. Arrange the tomatoes, artichoke hearts, olives, tofu, blistered green beans, and potatoes in neat piles on top. Sprinkle capers all over. Serve with extra dressing on the side, if desired.

CHARRED BROCCOLI CRUNCH SALAD

MAKES 4 TO 5 SERVINGS

Broccoli haters, prepare to be converted. Charred just to the cusp of being burnt, those crispy florets stay bright green and tender within, while boasting a bold smoky, almost nutty flavor. Tossed with all sorts of crunchy bites like crisp carrots, almonds, apples, and sunflower seeds, it's a riot of textures that positively dance across the tongue. Still think you don't like broccoli? Fire up the oven and think again.

2 medium crowns broccoli (about 5 cups florets)
2 tablespoons olive oil
1 medium red apple, cored and chopped
1 medium carrot, peeled and finely diced
1 small shallot, finely diced
½ cup toasted, unsalted almonds, roughly chopped
¼ cup toasted, unsalted sunflower seeds
¼ cup lemon juice
1 tablespoon maple syrup
1 tablespoon Dijon mustard
¼ teaspoon salt
¼ teaspoon pepper

Preheat your oven to 475°F.

On a lightly greased 11 × 17-inch sheet pan, spread the broccoli out in an even layer. Drizzle liberally with olive oil, rubbing it gently with your hands to fully coat each piece.

Place on the upper rack in the oven, bringing it as close to the heating element as possible, and roast for 25 minutes. Remove the pan and stir the broccoli to expose more of the undersides. Spread it back out into a single layer, overlapping florets as little as possible.

Return the sheet pan to the oven and roast for another 20 to 25 minutes. The edges of the florets will look alarmingly browned, very dark, almost to the point of being burnt; this is perfect.

Meanwhile, in a large bowl, toss together the chopped apple, carrot, shallot, almonds, and sunflower seeds. Separately, whisk together the lemon juice, maple syrup, Dijon mustard, salt, and pepper in a small dish to create the dressing; set aside.

Remove and transfer the broccoli to your bowl of crunchy vegetables. Add in the dressing, toss vigorously to coat, and serve immediately to enjoy warm. Alternately, chill the mixture in the fridge for at least an hour for a more refreshing, cold crunchy salad.

CRISPY KALE SALAD

MAKES 3 TO 4 SERVINGS

Kale chips are great in concept, but all too frequently fail to live up to their promise of crisp, cheesy goodness. The trouble is that kale has too many natural variations to cook evenly in home ovens, typically burning around the edges before the thicker centers can even soften. Take that into account, however, and you get the best kale salad you ever stuck a fork into. Served warm, the crunchy edges add satisfying texture contrast to the tender, gently wilted greens. Whereas it can be a struggle to get through a mountain of raw kale, you'll be able to polish off a full pound with ease given the sheet pan treatment.

⅓ cup creamy, unsweetened cashew butter
¼ cup nutritional yeast
1 clove garlic, minced
½ teaspoon salt
¼ teaspoon paprika
¼ cup lemon juice
¼ cup water
1 large bunch (about 1 pound) curly kale, stems removed and roughly torn
½ cup raw cashews, roughly chopped

Preheat your oven to 250°F. Line a half sheet pan with aluminum foil or parchment paper to prevent sticking. Set aside.

In a large bowl, mix the cashew butter, nutritional yeast, garlic, salt, and paprika until smooth. Slowly drizzle in the lemon juice and water while whisking. Once fully incorporated, add in the kale, stirring aggressively to coat. You might want to use your hands to mix and mash it around; you want to tenderize it a bit, and most importantly, get even coverage of all the leaves.

Transfer the dressed greens to your prepared sheet pan. Don't worry if you need to pile it up a bit, as long as the layer is even. Sprinkle the cashews over the top and slide the pan into the center of the oven.

Bake for 10 minutes. Stir thoroughly and set the broiler on high. Move the pan up to the top rack of the oven and cook for another 10 to 12 minutes, until crispy around the edges, wilted, and tender all the way through. Serve immediately.

CURRIED NAAN PANZANELLA

MAKES 4 TO 6 SERVINGS

Salads, by my estimation, can genuinely be anything tossed together in a bowl. Nothing is off limits; cooked grains, nuts, fruit, vegetables are all fair game of course, but what about that loaf of bread sitting on the counter, growing more stale by the hour? There's a long tradition of thrifty Italians inventing imaginative twists on panzanella, so that only stretches the imagination for the uninitiated. Expanding on that carb-based formula, consider the pita and all it does for fattoush over in the Middle East. Thus, it stands to reason that naan should be a perfectly acceptable ingredient in this formula as well, right?

Lightly toasting chewy naan bread to a crisp finish and anointing it with a golden curry dressing creates an unbeatable combination for summertime savoring, and well beyond. Feel free to expand upon the vegetable inclusions based on what you have available, or go crazy with your own creative add-ins. As we've established, a salad is anything you want it to be, if you just believe in it.

1 pound cherry or grape tomatoes, halved

1 English cucumber, quartered and sliced

1 teaspoon salt, divided

10–12 ounces (2 pieces) garlic naan bread, cut into 1-inch squares

5 tablespoons olive oil, divided

2 tablespoons lime juice

2 tablespoons tahini

2 teaspoons madras curry powder

¼ teaspoon ground black pepper

1 (14-ounce) can (1½ cups cooked) chickpeas, rinsed and drained

½ cup fresh cilantro, roughly chopped

Begin by tossing the sliced tomatoes and cucumbers with half of the salt. Set aside for about 15 minutes to draw out some of the excess liquid. Drain the extra water they've given off before proceeding.

Meanwhile, combine the sliced naan with 2 tablespoons of oil and spread the pieces out in an even layer on a half sheet pan. Run under the broiler in your oven set to high for 10 to 15 minutes, until toasted, golden brown, and crisp.

Simply whisk together the remaining oil, lime juice, tahini, curry powder, black pepper, and remaining salt to create the dressing. Toss everything into a large bowl, including the drained vegetables, toasted bread, dressing, chickpeas, and cilantro, and mix well to combine. Serve immediately; this salad doesn't keep well once dressed as the naan will begin to get soggy.

> If you can't find vegan naan, any other soft flatbread will do, such as pita, lavash, or even thick flour tortillas.

GREEK THREE-BEAN SALAD

MAKES 6 SERVINGS

Three-bean salad is a quintessential potluck staple. It's comforting, protein-rich, and easy to slap together in a hurry with basic pantry ingredients. The trouble is that most people just dump in cans of beans and run, without taking care to craft a more compelling story with their ingredients. Beyond beans, what makes this dish truly shine?

Greek herbs and spices infuse this simple vinaigrette, coating every little legume with a little taste of the islands. Fresh green beans soften in the oven amongst peppers and fennel, while cherry tomatoes burst with concentrated sweetness. Effectively evoking the nostalgic experience of eating an enormous leafy Greek salad at your favorite greasy spoon diner but condensing it into a contemporary family-style dish, there are never leftovers, no matter the number of eaters.

1½ cups (6 ounces) fresh green beans, cut into 1-inch lengths

½ medium red onion, thinly sliced

1 medium red bell pepper, seeded and cut into 1-inch strips

2 cups (10 ounces) cherry or grape tomatoes

1 small bulb fennel, fronds removed, halved, and thinly sliced

2 cloves garlic, minced

3 tablespoons olive oil

¼ teaspoon salt

¾ teaspoon dried oregano

½ teaspoon crushed red pepper flakes

1 (15-ounce) can red kidney beans, rinsed and drained

1 (15-ounce) can chickpeas, rinsed and drained

1 (14-ounce) can quartered artichoke hearts

½ cup pitted and sliced kalamata olives

3 tablespoons fresh dill, roughly chopped

2 tablespoons red wine vinegar

Preheat your oven to 375°F.

On a half sheet pan, toss together the green beans, onion, bell pepper, tomatoes, fennel, garlic, olive oil, and salt. Once well combined, spread them out in an even layer with the ingredients equally distributed across the sheet pan.

Roast on the top rack of your oven for 25 to 30 minutes, until the fennel is tender, and the tomatoes have burst. Pull the pan out and sprinkle evenly with oregano and red pepper flakes.

Meanwhile, in a large bowl, combine the kidney beans, chickpeas, artichokes, and olives, gently stirring with a wide spatula so as not to crush anything. Transfer the hot vegetables from the sheet pan to the bowl, along with the dill and vinegar. Mix just enough to incorporate.

Serve right away, while hot or at room temperature. This salad can also be prepared up to a day in advance and served chilled for a more refreshing experience.

PERFECT PICNIC POTATO SALAD

MAKES 6 TO 8 SERVINGS

No matter the occasion, no alfresco gathering is complete without an abundant bowl of potato salad. Velvety smooth, gently tangy dressing is whipped up using cream cheese in this rendition, allowing it to withstand the heat of midday sunshine without breaking or going bad.

POTATO SALAD:

¼ cup olive oil, divided

2 pounds Yukon gold potatoes, peeled and diced

1 small or ½ large red onion, quartered and sliced

2 cloves garlic, minced

½ teaspoon salt, divided

½ cup (4 ounces) vegan cream cheese

2 tablespoons apple cider vinegar

1 tablespoon lemon juice

1 tablespoon fresh or 1 teaspoon dried dill

1 tablespoon Dijon mustard

1 teaspoon celery seeds

¼ teaspoon ground black pepper

2 stalks celery, diced

2 scallions, thinly sliced

HARD BOILED TOFU:

4 ounces (¼ pound) super firm tofu, diced

2 teaspoons white or chickpea miso paste

½ teaspoon black salt (kala namak)

Preheat your oven to 425°F and line a half sheet pan with aluminum foil.

Toss the potatoes, onion, and garlic with 2 tablespoons of the oil and spread out in a single layer on the sheet pan. Sprinkle with half of the salt and bake for 25 to 35 minutes, stirring every 10 minutes or so, until the potatoes are tender, deeply browned, and lightly blistered on the outside. Let cool completely.

Meanwhile, beat the cream cheese in a large bowl until soft. Add the remaining salt along with the vinegar, lemon juice, dill, Dijon mustard, celery seeds, and black pepper. Whisk until completely smooth and creamy. Add in the celery, scallions, and cooled potatoes, tossing to coat.

For the hard-boiled tofu, simply stir together the tofu cubes with the miso and black salt until well combined. Try not to break up the tofu too much, but don't worry; some crumbling is inevitable.

Add the seasoned tofu and remaining 2 tablespoons of oil, toss lightly to combine, and chill for at least 2 to 3 hours before serving. The salad can be made up to 5 days in advance if stored in an airtight container in the fridge.

I have no rhythm and I can't dance, but I can certainly do the mashed potato! If you'd like to boogie with me, don't bother chilling the potatoes and simply toss them right in with the dressing while hot. Omit the celery, dill, and tofu. Mash along with 3 to 4 tablespoons of unsweetened non-dairy milk, until creamy and ready to lavish with gravy.

No peeler? No problem! Use diced red potatoes and roast them with the skins on.

PESTO TABBOULEH

MAKES 4 TO 6 SERVINGS

Tabbouleh is a staple for when the weather warms and gardens reawaken with a profusion of tender herbs. It's the simplest combination of fresh ingredients that absolutely screams summer! in every cool, refreshing bite. Tomatoes and parsley make up the foundation, with a handful of cracked wheat acting as the mortar holding everything together. Toss in a verdant bouquet of leafy basil, and suddenly you have a chunky, vegetable-heavy pesto you can eat with a fork.

1 pint cherry or grape tomatoes
3 tablespoons olive oil, divided
¾ teaspoon salt, divided
¼ teaspoon ground black pepper
1 cup coarse bulgur
3 cups water
1½ cups fresh basil, finely minced
1½ cups fresh parsley, finely minced
2 scallions, thinly sliced
¼ cup sundried tomatoes, julienned
¼ cup toasted pine nuts
2 tablespoons lemon juice

Preheat your oven to 450°F. On a quarter sheet pan, toss the tomatoes with 1 tablespoon of the olive oil, ¼ teaspoon of the salt, and pepper, and roast on bottom rack of oven until soft and skins have blistered and burst; 15 to 20 minutes.

Sprinkle bulgur on top and return to the oven without stirring. Cook for 10 minutes longer to lightly toast the bulgur. Carefully pour the water all over without removing the pan and continue to cook for an additional 12 to 15 minutes, until the liquid has been absorbed.

Let cool completely before transferring the bulgur mixture to a large bowl. Add the remaining oil and salt along with the basil, parsley, scallions, sundried tomatoes, pine nuts, and lemon juice. Toss thoroughly to combine.

Chill for at least an hour before serving to let the flavors mingle and meld. Stored in an airtight container in the fridge, the tabbouleh can be prepared up to 5 days in advance.

SOUTHWESTERN WEDGE SALAD

MAKES 4 SERVINGS

Iceberg lettuce gets a lot of shade as a bland, watery base for forgettable garden salads. It's an unfair assessment, passing harsh judgement on what a "good" leafy vegetable should be. In fact, some compositions can only shine with a crisp, juicy base that's otherwise silent to support brash, bold toppers that would otherwise clash. Wedge salad is the perfect example, where iceberg serves as the only suitable vehicle for such a cacophony of salty, crunchy, and crave-worthy star players. Rather than playing it safe with predictable bacon bits or ranch dressing, this same setup is primed for spicier flavors. A Tex-Mex combination of peppers, corn, avocado, and black beans all sizzle with a quietly smoldering heat perfectly match by that cool contender, sliced into hefty wedges that demand a knife and fork. Even if iceberg isn't much to munch on by itself, you'll want second servings when it's dressed up right.

SOUTHWESTERN SALAD:

2 teaspoons olive oil, divided
½ medium red bell pepper, seeded and diced
½ small jalapeño, seeded and diced
1 cup corn kernels, canned and drained or frozen and thawed
2 (4-inch) corn tortillas
½ teaspoon chili powder
¼ teaspoon salt
1 large head iceberg lettuce, quartered
1 medium avocado, pitted and diced
1 (14-ounce) can black beans, rinsed and drained

CHIPOTLE-YOGURT DRESSING:

½ cup plain, unsweetened vegan yogurt
1 canned chipotle in adobo, finely minced
1 tablespoon adobo sauce
1 tablespoon lime juice
2 cloves garlic, finely minced
½ teaspoon salt

Preheat your oven to 400°F. Line a half sheet pan with parchment paper or aluminum foil.

In a small bowl, toss together 1 teaspoon of the oil with the bell pepper, jalapeño, and corn. Once coated, spread the vegetables across half of the prepared sheet pan in an even layer; set aside.

Cut the tortillas into approximately ½-inch wide, 1½-inch-long strips. Toss the pieces with the remaining teaspoon of oil and chili powder. Spread the pieces out on the other side of the sheet pan, overlapping as little as possible. Sprinkle salt evenly over the whole sheet.

Slide the sheet pan into the oven on the highest rack. Bake for 10 minutes, flip the tortilla strips and stir the vegetables, and bake for another 5 to 15 minutes, until the tortillas are crisp, and the vegetables are lightly charred. Keep a close eye on the tortillas, as they may cook faster. If that's the case, transfer them to a plate before continuing to roast the corn and peppers further.

Meanwhile, prepare the dressing by combining the yogurt, chipotle and adobo sauce, lime juice, garlic, and salt in a small bowl. Stir thoroughly to incorporate all the ingredients.

To assemble, place ¼ head of lettuce on each plate. Drizzle ¼ of the dressing over each wedge, followed by equal amounts of the roasted vegetables, diced avocado, and black beans. Serve right away, while the vegetables are still warm, and the lettuce is cool and crisp.

TOFU CAPRESE

MAKES 4 SERVINGS

A study in simplicity, caprese is an elegant solution to seasonal eating that needs no further explanation. The Italians nailed the concept hundreds of years ago without ever writing down a recipe. Soft cheese, tomatoes, basil, and salt are at the heart of this soulful salad, the whole of which is greater than its parts. Still, there's always room for improvement, especially by applying a kiss of heat, a touch of sharp vinegar, and soft tofu for unexpected umami. Curd nerds will cry foul at the removal of mozzarella, but I promise, you'll never miss it when you have blistered, bursting tomatoes and silky soy melting on your tongue instead.

1 (12-ounce) aseptic package extra-firm silken tofu
1½ pounds grape or cherry tomatoes
3 tablespoons olive oil
2 tablespoons balsamic vinegar
½ teaspoon salt
¼ teaspoon ground black pepper
½ cup fresh basil leaves, roughly torn or sliced

Preheat your oven to 425°F. Line a half sheet pan with aluminum foil if desired, for easier cleanup.

Handling the tofu very gently so as not to break it up, slice it in half lengthwise and cut into ½-inch cubes. The curds are quite soft and delicate, so it helps to use a flat spatula to transfer the pieces to your prepared sheet pan. Spread them out in a single layer and add the cherry tomatoes to the mix. Drizzle evenly with olive oil and vinegar, and sprinkle with salt and pepper.

Roast in the center of the oven until the tomatoes are a bit wrinkled, blistered, and just starting to char; about 30 to 35 minutes.

Remove and let cool for 15 minutes. Transfer to a platter or bowl along with any excess juices. Add fresh basil and toss very, very gently to combine. Serve right away while still warm or refrigerate for up to 8 hours to enjoy chilled.

WARM BRUSSELS SPROUTS SALAD

MAKES 4 TO 6 SERVINGS

Like mashed potatoes and gravy, roasted Brussels sprouts are an indispensable addition to any festive holiday meal. Shredding those sprouts creates a more consistent caramelized surface, yielding more of that addictive crunchy texture everyone loves. Coated in a sweet-tart-tangy marinade with earthy notes of thyme and sage, this is the ultimate expression of autumn itself. Smoky coconut bacon and crisp toasted hazelnuts punctuate every forkful with a salty, savory exclamation point. Invite this warm, charming tangle of greens to Thanksgiving if you want to really impress your parents.

COCONUT BACON:

4 teaspoons soy sauce
1½ teaspoons liquid smoke
1½ teaspoons maple syrup
1½ teaspoons olive oil
⅛ teaspoon ground black pepper
1 cup large coconut chips or flakes

BRUSSELS SPROUTS SALAD:

¼ cup olive oil
2 tablespoons apple cider vinegar
1 tablespoon apple butter
1 teaspoon dried thyme
¼ teaspoon dried sage, crumbled
¼ teaspoon crushed red pepper
    flakes
¼ teaspoon salt
1 pound Brussels sprouts, finely
    shredded (about 8 cups)
½ cup toasted hazelnuts, roughly
    chopped

Preheat your oven to 300°F and line a half sheet pan with parchment paper or a silicone baking mat.

Stir together the soy sauce, liquid smoke, maple syrup, oil, and pepper in a large mixing bowl. Toss the coconut in and stir with a wide spatula, coating the flakes thoroughly with the liquids. Be gentle to prevent the coconut from breaking into small pieces.

Pour everything, including any excess marinade, into your waiting pan. Bake for about 28 to 32 minutes, stirring every 10 minutes or so to keep the entire batch cooking evenly. The flakes can burn very easily and surprisingly quickly, so stand by and keep a close eye on it the entire time it's in the oven. Cook until deeply browned all over and highly aromatic. Remove the sheet pan from the oven and turn on the broiler to high.

Meanwhile, in a medium bowl, whisk together the oil, vinegar, apple butter, thyme, sage, red pepper flakes, and salt. Set aside.

Spread the shredded Brussels sprouts on top of the coconut bacon, completely covering it. Keep the sprouts in as even a layer as possible to maximize the exposed surface area. Return the sheet pan to the oven, placing it on the upper rack to bring it closer to the broiler. Cook for 5 minutes, until very lightly browned around the edges.

Quickly transfer the warm sprouts and coconut bacon to a large bowl, using the parchment or silicone mat as a sling to easily lift everything off the tray and funnel it into the vessel. Drizzle with the dressing and toss thoroughly to combine. Top with toasted hazelnuts and serve immediately.

There's more than one way to shave a sprout! My favorite method employs a mandoline set to slice at 1mm thickness. Use a fork to firmly skewer a sprout from the bottom and shave away, without risking your fingertips at the same time. If you have a food processor, you can make very quick work out of it using the slicing blade, too; just make sure you trim the ends and very thoroughly clean them first. Finally, it doesn't require fancy equipment for the most basic approach. Just use a very sharp knife and arm yourself with a heaping helping of patience.

SIDES

BABY CORN ESQUITES

MAKES 4 TO 6 SERVINGS

Elote, otherwise known as Mexican street corn, get all the glory for their easy grab-and-go format, but personally, I quite prefer esquites. It's the same concept, but with the kernels cut off the cob, which makes it considerably less messy to eat. Prep work becomes a bit fussier though, so using baby corn is the best of both worlds. You get to eat the whole thing, there's no annoying knifework, and you get a rich, cheesy, creamy warm snack to dig into almost instantly. You'll never be able to go back to the conventional approach after firing up the oven!

2 (15-ounce) cans whole baby corn
¼ cup vegan mayonnaise
1 teaspoon hot sauce, such as Tabasco
  or Cholula
2 tablespoons lime juice
½ teaspoon ground cumin
½ teaspoon salt
¼ cup nutritional yeast or vegan
  Parmesan shreds
2 tablespoons fresh cilantro, minced
Chili powder, to taste

Thoroughly drain your cans of baby corn and spread them out in an even layer on a half sheet pan. Place the pan on the upper rack of your oven and set the broiler on high. Broil for 10 to 15 minutes, stirring halfway through, until the baby corn is lightly charred all over.

Transfer the charred corn to a large bowl. Add the mayonnaise, hot sauce, lime juice, cumin, salt, and nutritional yeast or Parmesan. Stir thoroughly to combine.

Transfer to a serving bowl or individual plates, and top with cilantro and chili powder, to taste. Enjoy hot or warm!

BROILED BHINDI MASALA

MAKES 3 TO 4 SERVINGS

Okra gets a bad rap for being slimy, but that's a shortcoming easily managed by proper cookery. Taking my favorite Indian curry featuring these green pods and converting it to sheet pan prep, the large surface area of the pan and the overhead heat sears the okra lightning fast, without stewing or braising in excess liquid. Adding cherry tomatoes for the last few minutes of cooking gives them time to soften without encouraging that gooey sauce to develop. Even if you haven't liked okra in the past, give them another chance with this sizzling, spicy dish!

2 tablespoons oil, divided
1 small red onion, quartered and
    sliced
¾ pound (about 3 cups) fresh okra
¾ teaspoon ground turmeric
¾ teaspoon ground cumin
¾ teaspoon ground coriander
½ teaspoon salt
¼ teaspoon cayenne pepper
1 cup cherry or grape tomatoes,
    halved
2 tablespoons lemon juice
¼ cup fresh cilantro or parsley,
    minced

Adjust the upper oven rack to rest about 5 inches away from the top element. It should be close enough to benefit from the intense, direct heat, but not so close that everything is instantly incinerated.

Preheat your oven with the broiler set to high and line a sheet pan with parchment paper or a silicone baking mat.

Drizzle 1 tablespoon of the oil over the lined baking sheet and distribute the sliced onion on top. Spread the whole okra pods out over the onions without mixing. Slide the pan into the oven and broil for 15 minutes, undisturbed.

Remove the sheet and sprinkle evenly with turmeric, cumin, coriander, salt, and cayenne. Still, resist the urge to stir and leave it be! Scatter the halved tomatoes on top, and drizzle with the remaining tablespoon of oil. Return it to the oven and broil for another 10 minutes.

Now, you can finally stir, mixing well to incorporate all the spices. Broil for a final 5 minutes, until the okra is nicely charred, and the tomatoes are slightly shriveled.

Drizzle with lemon juice and toss to coat. Transfer to a serving dish and top with minced herbs. Enjoy hot, alongside flatbread, cooked rice, or all by itself.

> To pump up the protein and make this a complete meal in one, incorporate 1 can of chickpeas, drained, in the final 5 minutes of cooking. The chickpeas should be warmed through and coated with that luscious spice mixture for a seamless addition.

CORN PUDDING

MAKES 10 TO 12 SERVINGS

Served warm to combat the chill of colder seasons, corn pudding is a staple at Southern Thanksgiving and Christmas celebrations. It's typically classified as a casserole or hotdish, right at home alongside the stuffing and green beans, though this rich custard is sometimes sweet enough to qualify as dessert. I prefer to go easy on the sugar, saving that for the pies instead. Baking it on a sheet pan creates thin sheets of fluffy, tender creamed corn with a bit more bite. Fresh is always best, but in the winter, frozen or canned is still quite a satisfying surrogate.

½ cup chickpea flour
½ cup coarse yellow cornmeal
2 teaspoons baking powder
1½ teaspoons salt
¼ teaspoon ground black pepper
1 cup plain, unsweetened vegan yogurt
½ cup full-fat coconut milk
½ cup coconut oil, melted
2 tablespoons maple syrup
6 cups (4 cans, drained, or 12 ears, shucked) corn kernels

Preheat your oven to 350°F. Lightly grease a half sheet pan or 2 quarter sheet pans and set aside.

In a medium bowl, whisk together the chickpea flour, cornmeal, baking powder, salt, and pepper. Separately, mix the yogurt, coconut milk, melted coconut oil, and maple syrup. Once smooth, add the liquid ingredients into the dry, and stir well to combine. No need to worry about over-mixing, as the batter is gluten-free! Give it a good beating to make sure there are no lumps.

Incorporate the corn kernels last and transfer to your prepared sheet pan(s). Spread out in an even layer and bake for 45 to 60 minutes, until set in the center and golden brown around the edges. Let cool for at least 15 minutes before serving. Enjoy hot or at room temperature.

> **Try using roasted corn kernels (available frozen) for extra smoky, charred flavor.**

JALAPEÑO CORNBREAD

MAKES 16 SERVINGS

Cornbread, soft and sweet, haunts my dreams. An impossibly dense yet fluffy crumb that melts away into a light, satisfyingly coarse grit on the tongue, this is the stuff of legends, made up of memories logged long ago during formative years that lack clear timestamps. It wasn't any old Jiffy mix calling to me from beyond the periphery of cognition. It was cornbread you eat as an event by itself, not a mere side dish to a grander spread; cornbread that stole the show. The gentle bite of jalapeños rings clearly throughout the golden yellow slab, dancing that fine line between dinner and dessert. For that matter, there's no shame in saving leftovers for breakfast, pan-seared and drizzled with maple syrup, too.

2 cups all-purpose flour

2 cups coarsely ground yellow
  cornmeal

2 teaspoons baking powder

1 teaspoon baking soda

1 teaspoon salt

2 jalapeños, divided

1 (14-ounce) can (1½ cups kernels)
  corn, drained

2 cups plain non-dairy milk

1 cup olive oil

½ cup unsweetened applesauce

½ cup light brown sugar, firmly
  packed

1 tablespoon lemon juice

Preheat your oven to 350°F and lightly grease a half sheet pan; set aside.

In a large bowl, mix the flour, cornmeal, baking powder and soda, and salt, stirring to thoroughly combine. Seed and diced one of the jalapeños and toss it in along with the corn kernels. Mix lightly to coat the vegetables with flour, which will help prevent them from sinking to the bottom during the baking process.

Separately, whisk together the non-dairy milk, olive oil, applesauce, brown sugar, and lemon juice. Once smooth, pour the liquid mixture into the bowl of dry ingredients, and use a wide spatula to gently incorporate. It's perfectly fine to leave a few errant lumps in the matrix.

Pour the batter into the prepared sheet pan. Thinly slice the remaining jalapeño and scatter the rings evenly across the top.

Bake for 25 to 30 minutes, until a toothpick inserted in the center comes out clean. Let cool for at least 20 to 30 minutes before slicing and serving, if you can bear the wait. It's also fabulous at room temperature and can keep for 3 to 4 days if kept sealed in an airtight container at room temperature, or up to a week in the fridge.

MELTING ZA'ATAR POTATOES

MAKES 6 TO 8 SERVINGS

Sliced into thick rounds, blasted with high heat, and bathed in a luxurious broth with za'atar spices, humble spuds transform into tender, buttery morsels that positively melt in your mouth. Basic roasted potatoes pale in comparison; these are downright juicy, succulent in a way that you might not expect from a starchy vegetable. Keep the entrée relatively simple because this side dish will easily steal the show.

¼ cup olive oil
2 tablespoons fresh thyme, divided
2 teaspoons toasted sesame seeds
1 teaspoon ground cumin
1 teaspoon ground coriander
1 teaspoon sumac
½ teaspoon salt
½ teaspoon ground black pepper
¼ teaspoon cayenne pepper
2 pounds Yukon gold potatoes, sliced
    into 1-inch rounds
4 cloves garlic, sliced
½ cup low-sodium vegetable stock
¼ cup lemon juice

Preheat your oven to 475°F.

In a large bowl, whisk together the olive oil, 1½ tablespoons thyme, sesame seeds, cumin, coriander, sumac, salt, black pepper, and cayenne. Add the potatoes and garlic, tossing to coat.

Transfer everything to a half sheet pan, spreading the potatoes out into one even layer. You need full contact to maximize the browning potential for your spuds. Try to arrange the garlic pieces on top of the potatoes, rather than the sheet pan itself, to prevent them from burning.

Roast for 15 minutes before removing the pan from the oven. Use a thin, flexible spatula to gently flip the potatoes. Remove and reserve any garlic that threatens to overcook. Return the sheet to the oven and roast for another 15 minutes.

The potatoes should start to look nice and toasty around the edges at this point. Carefully pour the stock and lemon juice all around the spuds, standing back as it may sputter and splatter a bit.

Roast for a final 12 to 15 more minutes, until the potatoes are meltingly tender, and the liquid has been absorbed. Top with the remaining fresh thyme and serve hot.

> **If you have ready-made za'atar seasoning, you're good to go! Simply use 3 to 4 tablespoons of the blend instead of the individual herbs and spices listed.**

MISO-GINGER GLAZED CARROTS

MAKES 6 TO 8 SERVINGS

Coaxing the inherent sweetness out of baby carrots doesn't take much extra work with the kiss of a hot oven concentrating the natural sugars within, while a brown sugar marinade infuses a molasses-like warmth from the outside. White miso is your secret ingredient, adding umami and a touch of salt to amplify that symphony of flavors. Bright, fresh ginger cuts through all the noise to end on a strong note that will continue reverberating long after the curtains for this meal are drawn.

2 pounds baby carrots, cut diagonally into ¼-inch-thick slices
¼ cup coconut oil, melted
¼ cup dark brown sugar, firmly packed
4 teaspoons fresh ginger, finely minced
¼ cup white miso paste
2 tablespoons water
1 scallion, thinly sliced

Preheat your oven to 425°F.

In a large bowl, toss together the carrots, coconut oil, brown sugar, and ginger. Once thoroughly coated, spread the carrots out on a half sheet pan in an even layer, without overlapping.

Cook for 10 minutes and stir well. In a separate dish, whisk together the miso paste with the water before pouring it all over the vegetables, mixing to incorporate. Bake for another 8 to 10 minutes, until the sauce has reduced to a thick caramel that clings richly to the carrots and the carrots are fork-tender.

Transfer to a serving plate and sprinkle with sliced scallion. Enjoy hot.

NUTHOUSE STUFFING

MAKES 8 TO 12 SERVINGS

If having the whole family over for holiday dinner makes you feel a bit nuts, you're not alone! 'Tis the season to get a bit nutty, especially for the main meal at hand. The sheer number of almonds, pecans and peanuts tumbling throughout this rich bread stuffing is downright bonkers. Don't be afraid to go crazy with your favorite blend; walnuts, pistachios, and hazelnuts are all welcome at this party, too! If you're going to spend time in the nuthouse, you might as well embrace every last goober and seed.

1 pound (about 10 cups) sourdough, French bread, or baguette, cut into ½-inch cubes
1 cup raw almonds
½ cup raw pecans
½ cup raw peanuts
6 tablespoons vegan butter or coconut oil, melted and divided
3 stalks celery, diced
1 medium yellow onion, diced
1 pound (about 2 large) sweet apples, such as fuji, braeburn, or honeycrisp, cored and diced
1 tablespoon fresh rosemary, minced
1 tablespoon fresh sage, minced
½ teaspoon dried thyme
1 teaspoon salt
2 cups vegetable stock, divided

Preheat your oven to 350°F and scatter the bread cubes on top of a half sheet pan, spreading the pieces out evenly. Toast for 10 minutes before adding the nuts and return to the oven for 8 to 10 minutes longer, until crisp and golden brown around the edges. Everything should smell perfectly, well, nutty!

Toss the celery, onion, and apples with 2 tablespoons of the melted butter or oil before layering the mixture right on top. Bake for 15 minutes, stirring halfway through.

Pull the sheet out to sprinkle the rosemary, sage, thyme, and salt all over. Drizzle with the remaining butter or oil, followed by the vegetable stock. Give it a good stir to combine before covering the pan with aluminum foil. Bake for 15 minutes, uncover, stir again, and cook for a final 10 to 15 minutes, until the bread is all golden-brown and the liquid has fully absorbed. You don't want the mixture to be dry, but it shouldn't be soupy either.

Transfer to a large bowl or casserole dish and serve hot, to all your favorite nutcases.

PUMPKIN PARKER HOUSE ROLLS

MAKES ABOUT 30 ROLLS

Classic Parker House Rolls are legendary; a buttery sheen highlights the voluptuous curves of their crisp crusts, concealing a tender, fluffy crumb within. They're as close to perfect as any dinner roll can come, right at home next to a steaming bowlful of chowder, sopping up the last drops of gravy, or slathered in jam. Originally crafted at the Boston Parker House Hotel in the 1870s, those early buns have nothing on this pumpkin-packed dough. Though it makes a large batch, they disappear in the blink of an eye, so you won't want to scale down this winning recipe.

1½ cups plain non-dairy milk, warmed to room temperature

¼ cup dark brown sugar, firmly packed, or coconut sugar

1 (¼-ounce) packet (1¾ teaspoons) active dry yeast

½ cup plus 2 tablespoons vegan butter, divided

¾ cup pumpkin puree

⅓ cup aquafaba

1½ teaspoons salt

6½–7½ cups all-purpose flour, divided

1 tablespoon fresh rosemary, roughly chopped

1 tablespoon fresh thyme, roughly chopped

1 tablespoon fresh parsley, roughly chopped

Coarse or flaky sea salt, to garnish (optional)

These rolls can be baked up to 5 days in advance. Wrap tightly in plastic and refrigerate until ready to serve. To reheat, unwrap and warm them in a 300°F oven for about 10 minutes. Brush with additional melted butter, as needed.

In a medium bowl, combine the non-dairy milk, sugar, and yeast. Let stand for 10 to 15 minutes, until the yeast reactivates and becomes slightly frothy.

Melt ¼ cup of the butter and place it in the bowl of your stand mixer, along with the pumpkin puree, aquafaba, salt, 3 cups of the flour, and milk mixture. Install the dough hook and begin mixing on low speed until combined. Pause to scrape down the bowl with your spatula as needed, to make sure everything is smoothly incorporated.

Add the remaining flour, ½ cup at a time, until dough comes together and forms a soft, smooth ball. Continue to knead with the dough hook for about 10 minutes. The dough should be elastic but not wet or sticky.

Transfer to a lightly greased bowl and cover with a clean kitchen towel. Let rest in a warm, draft-free place for about an hour, or until roughly doubled in size.

Preheat your oven to 350°F.

On a lightly floured surface, roll out the dough to ½-inch in thickness; the overall shape isn't terribly important. Use a 2½-inch round cookie cutter to stamp out the individual rolls. If the dough is sticking to the sides, dip the cookie cutter in flour first, to coat the edges.

Melt the remaining butter and brush it over the top of each round. Fold the rounds in half before placing them on a half sheet pan, lined up evenly and just barely touching. They will continue to rise and expand to fill the space. Repeat, gathering up the scraps and re-rolling, until all the dough is used. Let rise for another 20 to 30 minutes.

Sprinkle the chopped rosemary, thyme, and parsley all over the top before sliding the pan into the oven. Bake for 25 to 30 minutes, until golden-brown all over. Finish with a light sprinkle of coarse or flaky salt, if desired. Serve warm.

SAUERKRAUT COLCANNON

MAKES 4 TO 6 SERVINGS

Call it pantry colcannon; instead of fresh cabbage, pleasantly tangy, satisfyingly salty sauerkraut gets mashed into the buttery potato mix instead. Possibly an upgrade on the classic Irish staple, it's a probiotic powerhouse, too.

6 tablespoons olive oil, divided
2 pounds Yukon gold potatoes, diced
1 medium yellow onion, diced
2 cloves garlic, minced
¼ cup water
2 cups sauerkraut, drained
1⅓ cups unsweetened non-dairy milk
½ teaspoon salt
½ teaspoon ground black pepper
3 tablespoons fresh parsley, minced

Preheat your oven to 350°F and coat the bottom of a half sheet pan with 1 tablespoon of oil. Scatter the potatoes on top, along with the onion and garlic, distributing the ingredients equally across the pan. Drizzle with 2 tablespoons of oil before sliding the pan into the oven.

Bake for 12 to 15 minutes, until the onions are translucent and beginning to brown around the edges. Drain thoroughly.

Add the water to steam the potatoes and make sure they cook all the way through. Return to the oven and bake for another 10 minutes or so, until the potatoes are fork tender.

Place the sauerkraut on top, followed by a drizzle of 1 tablespoon of oil, and cook for just 2 to 3 minutes longer, to warm all the way through.

Transfer the cooked vegetable mixture to a large bowl and pour in the non-dairy milk. Season with salt, pepper, and parsley. Roughly mash with a potato masher, until it reaches your desired consistency.

Drizzle with the remaining olive oil right before serving.

SCALLOPED SUMMER SQUASH

MAKES 6 TO 8 SERVINGS

If you're growing zucchini or yellow crookneck squash in your backyard garden, there's a good chance that you're up to your ears in gourds by the time July rolls around. Common weeds aren't as vigorous, crowded out by masses of tangled vines heavy with fruit and flowers. When you've had your fill of zucchini bread and can't stomach another pile of spiralized zoodles, try this elegant solution, complete with an effortless creamy, cheesy sauce. Baking it in a sheet pan rather than a casserole ensures that all the vegetables retain their structure, rather than turning into soft, soupy morass. Soon you'll wish you had even more squash to contend with.

¼ cup vegan butter
½ medium yellow onion, halved and thinly sliced
4 cloves garlic, minced
1 pound (2 medium) zucchini
1 pound (2 medium) yellow squash
¼ cup nutritional yeast
2 tablespoons tapioca starch
1 tablespoon dried parsley
½ teaspoon salt
½ teaspoon dried oregano
¼ teaspoon smoked paprika
⅛ teaspoon ground black pepper
2 cups plain, unsweetened non-dairy milk
2 tablespoons fresh basil

Preheat your oven to 400°F and place the butter in a half sheet pan. Set it in the oven and allow it to melt while preheating.

Add the onion and garlic, stir to combine, and return it to the oven. Bake on the center rack for 6 to 8 minutes, until aromatic and lightly browned.

Meanwhile, use a mandoline or very sharp knife to slice the zucchini and yellow squash as thinly as possible; ideally about ⅛-inch thick. Place the cut vegetables in a large bowl and add the nutritional yeast, starch, parsley, salt, oregano, paprika, and pepper, tossing to coat.

Arrange the seasoned squash in slightly overlapping rows in the baking sheet, on top of the browned aromatics. Slowly pour the non-dairy milk on top, drizzling it evenly over everything.

Bake in the center of your oven for 25 to 30 minutes, until lightly browned, bubbly, and the squash are fork tender. Let cool for at least 10 minutes, garnish with fresh basil, and serve hot.

SNAPPY SNAP PEA RISOTTO

MAKES 3 TO 4 SERVINGS

Anyone that tells you risotto demands constant attention, relentless stirring and coddling over a hot stove for ages, is either misinformed or trying to keep a secret. The truth is that it doesn't take much work to create ideally al dente yet creamy rice, despite its reputation as a finicky dish. Take a low-impact approach and let the starchy rice itself do the heavy lifting, all while supporting crisp pods of sugar snap peas, with fresh lemon and cracked pepper for brightness. This fresh approach to risotto makes it as easy to prepare as it is to eat.

3 tablespoons olive oil
1 leek, halved, cleaned, and sliced
3 cloves garlic, thinly sliced
½ teaspoon salt
¼ cup dry white wine
1 cup arborio rice
2 dried shiitake mushrooms, crumbled or finely minced
3½–4 cups vegetable stock, divided
½ pound sugar snap peas
½ cup green peas, fresh or frozen and thawed
3 tablespoons nutritional yeast
2 tablespoons lemon juice
¼ teaspoon ground black pepper
¼ cup fresh parsley, minced

> **Celebrate all the bounty of spring with a wider array of tender green vegetables. Try using fresh fava beans instead of peas, add asparagus, or branch out with delicate pea shoots mixed in right at the very end.**

Adjust your oven rack to the middle position and preheat to 400°F. It may sound excessively hot, but since you need to open and close the door frequently, the actual temperature will fall well below that.

Drizzle the olive oil generously over a half sheet pan. Add the leek, garlic, and salt, tossing lightly to coat and combine. Roast, stirring once about halfway through the cooking process, until tender and aromatic; about 10 minutes.

Gently pour the wine on top and return the pan to the oven for 5 minutes. Very carefully, clad in oven mitts, pull the oven rack out partway and stir in the rice and dried shiitake mushrooms. Slide the rack back into place and continue to bake for 5 minutes.

Pull out the oven rack partway again and stir 1 cup of the vegetable stock into the rice. Carefully slide the rack back into place and bake until the liquid is mostly absorbed, about 8 to 10 minutes. Pull out the oven rack partway and stir in another 1½ cups broth. Carefully slide the rack back into place and bake for 8 to 10 minutes more. The rice will begin to swell and absorb most of the liquid.

Pull the rack out partway once more and carefully stir in 1 more cup of stock, along with the snap peas. Bake 8 to 10 minutes further, until the rice is plump, creamy, and al dente. Add up to ½ cup more stock if needed to achieve the perfect consistency.

Remove the sheet pan completely and mix in the green peas, nutritional yeast, and lemon juice. Let rest for 5 minutes for the rice to finish cooking and fully drink in all the stock. Add the ground black pepper and parsley and serve piping hot.

SPICY SICHUAN SNOW PEAS

MAKES 3 TO 4 SERVINGS

Thick or thin, long or short, pea pods are cherished as harbingers of spring the world over. In China, they can also symbolize unity, containing multiple unique seeds in one vegetal pouch. Eaten all together, they're best prepared as a flash in the pan. Cooked any longer, they'd decompose into murky brown sludge. That's why these spicy snow peas take mere minutes to make in a simple Sichuan-style glaze. Bold, savory, with a mouth-tingling kick, Sichuan peppercorns are essential for creating what's known as mala taste. There's no mistaking or replacing this pungent blend of chiles, vinegar, soy, and subtle sweetness. Yes, it's spicy, but there's so much more to it than that. Complex layers of flavors that involve all the senses; it's a full visceral experience, so much as it is a taste.

1 pound fresh snow peas
2 tablespoons peanut oil or avocado oil
2 tablespoons fermented black beans
2 tablespoons Shaoxing rice wine or dry sherry
1 tablespoon soy sauce
1 teaspoon dark brown sugar or coconut sugar
½ teaspoon salt
1 teaspoon whole Sichuan peppercorns
4 whole dried red chilies or 1 teaspoon crushed red pepper flakes
3 cloves garlic, minced
1 teaspoon fresh ginger, finely minced

Adjust the top rack in your oven to the highest position and preheat the broiler to high and line a half sheet pan with aluminum foil or parchment paper.

In a large bowl, toss all the ingredients together to thoroughly combine, completely coating the snow peas in seasonings. Arrange the vegetables in a single layer on prepared sheet pan and slide it into the oven. Broil until the pods are bright green, blistered, and very lightly charred; 2 to 5 minutes depending on the intensity and distance of the broiler.

Pull out the whole chilies or simply pick around them when serving. Enjoy immediately.

STEAKHOUSE CABBAGE WITH HORSERADISH CREAM

MAKES 4 TO 5 SERVINGS

Maybe I'm secretly a rabbit dressed up like a human, but I love cabbage. To treat it right, cut a tightly packed head into thick slabs, toss it in the oven, and let the edges get all golden and caramelized. It's disturbingly easy to eat a whole pound with this simple treatment. Serve with creamy, peppery horseradish sauce, and you might just get in touch with your inner rabbit, too.

CABBAGE STEAKS:
2 tablespoons olive oil, divided
1 medium head (about 3 pounds)
   green or red cabbage
½ teaspoon flaky or coarse salt
½ teaspoon whole black peppercorns,
   roughly crushed

HORSERADISH CREAM SAUCE:
½ cup vegan sour cream
2 tablespoons prepared horseradish
1 tablespoon apple cider vinegar
¼ teaspoon salt
⅛ teaspoon ground black pepper

Preheat your oven to 400°F. Coat a half sheet pan with 1 tablespoon of the olive oil.

Use a very sharp knife to cut the cabbage into 1-inch-thick slabs. Arrange the "steaks" in a single layer on your prepared sheet, wedging them in to fit as needed. Brush with the remaining tablespoon of oil before sprinkling evenly with salt and pepper.

Roast for 45 to 55 minutes, until the cabbage is tender throughout and the edges are caramelized.

Meanwhile, prepare the sauce by simply whisking together the sour cream, horseradish, vinegar, salt, and pepper until smooth.

Serve the cabbage steaks piping hot, drizzled with horseradish cream sauce, or plated alongside for dipping, as desired.

SOUPS & STEWS

CANH CHUA

MAKES 4 TO 6 SERVINGS

Hot and sour soup is most commonly associated with Chinese cuisine, but the Vietnamese have a sweet twist on this pungent brew. It doesn't show up on many menus because it's a simpler, homemade dish without a claim to fame abroad. There are as many variations of canh chua as there are cooks that make it. Tomatoes, pineapple, and tamarind are mandatory to form the characteristic tangy, tart, and sweet base, but all the rest is optional; mix and match vegetables however your heart desires. Add steaming hot white rice, and you have yourself a complete meal.

3 tablespoons avocado, peanut, or olive oil, divided
10 cloves garlic
¼ teaspoon salt
8 ounces extra-firm tofu, cut into ½-inch cubes
½ pound okra, sliced into ½-inch chunks
2 Roma tomatoes (about ¾ pound), halved and cut into ¼-inch wedges
1 cup crushed pineapple, canned in 100% pineapple juice, undrained
2 tablespoons tomato paste
2 tablespoons lime juice
1 tablespoon lemongrass paste or puree
1 tablespoon soy sauce
1 tablespoon coconut sugar or dark brown sugar, firmly packed
¼ cup fresh basil, julienned
4–6 cups vegetable stock, hot sriracha, to taste (optional)

Enjoy this soup as a hearty starter or make it a more substantial meal by adding hot sticky rice or rice noodles!

Preheat your oven to 350°F and line a quarter sheet pan with parchment paper. Drizzle with 1 tablespoon of the oil and rub it evenly over the paper.

Slice the garlic cloves as thinly and consistently as possible. It's important to keep them all the same thickness so they cook at the same rate, without getting burnt or undercooked in different spots. Lay the pieces out in an even layer without overlapping, and drizzle with another tablespoon of oil. Sprinkle evenly with salt.

Bake until golden brown all over; 10 to 15 minutes. Keep a close eye on the garlic chips because they'll go from lightly caramelized to completely incinerated very quickly. Remove the sheet of garlic from the pan and let cool.

Meanwhile, line a half sheet pan with a silicone baking mat or piece of parchment paper and set aside. Spread the tofu cubes out in an even layer on one side of the pan. Place the sliced okra and tomatoes alongside, and drizzle everything with the remaining tablespoon of oil.

Bake for 25 to 30 minutes, until the tofu is lightly golden around the edges.

In a separate bowl, combine the crushed pineapple, tomato paste, lime juice, lemongrass, soy sauce, and sugar. Once thoroughly blended, with no big clumps remaining, pour the mixture all over the tofu and vegetables. Cook for 5 minutes, to heat through. Scrape the bottom of the pan with a spatula to make sure nothing sticks and gets left behind.

Carefully remove the pan from the oven and stir in the fresh basil and half of the garlic chips. Divide between 4 to 6 bowls and top each with 1 cup of hot vegetable stock. Garnish with the remaining garlic chips and sriracha, if desired.

CHAMPIONSHIP FOUR-PEPPER CHILI

MAKE 6 TO 8 SERVINGS

Ring the alarm bell; this fiery chili will set your mouth ablaze! That alarm system comes from the storied firehouse meal, frequently a large bubbling cauldron of meat, beans, and vegetables that can be made in bulk and simmered all day, ready to feed a company of hungry firefighters whenever they might have time to pause for a meal. The number of alarms is correlated to how many fire engines would be needed to put out a fire; a more intense inferno demanding more trucks are deployed. Before long, that same system of measurement came to apply the spicy chili bubbling away in the kitchen, too. This particular blend isn't quite so alarming, featuring sweeter peppers to emphasize flavor over pure fire power. Feel free to pump up the heat with extra hot sauce if you really want to feel the burn.

CHILI:
2 tablespoons olive oil
1 medium yellow onion, diced
2 cloves garlic, minced
1 teaspoon salt, divided
½ pound cremini or button
    mushrooms, roughly chopped
1 red, orange, or yellow bell pepper,
    seeded and diced
1 poblano pepper, seeded and diced
1 cubanelle pepper, seeded and diced
1 jalapeño pepper, seeded and diced
2 tablespoons chili powder
2 tablespoons coconut sugar or dark
    brown sugar, firmly packed
1 tablespoon Dutch-process cocoa
    powder
1 teaspoon instant coffee
1 teaspoon dried basil
1 teaspoon dried oregano
1 teaspoon smoked paprika
½ teaspoon ground black pepper
½ teaspoon liquid smoke
2 (14.5-ounce) cans fire-roasted diced
    tomatoes
2 tablespoons tomato paste
1 cup mushroom or vegetable stock
⅓ cup dry bulgur
1 (15-ounce) can black beans, drained
    and rinsed

TO SERVE:
Diced avocado
Thinly sliced scallions

Preheat your oven to 350°F.

On a half sheet pan, toss the onion with the oil, garlic, and ½ teaspoon of the salt. Roast in the middle of the preheated oven until the onion is fragrant and softened; about 8 to 10 minutes.

Add the mushrooms and peppers before returning the sheet to the oven, and bake for another 10 minutes, until the vegetables are tender. Sprinkle in the chili powder, sugar, cocoa, instant coffee, dried basil, oregano, paprika, and pepper, stirring well to combine. Bake for another 10 minutes.

Remove the baking sheet from the oven before carefully adding the liquid smoke and tomatoes, along with the liquid in the can. Whisk the tomato paste into the stock, making sure it's fully dissolved before gently pouring it over the vegetables. Add the bulgur last, making sure all the granules are fully submerged.

Reduce the heat to 325°F and cook for about 20 to 30 minutes, until the excess liquid has been absorbed and the bulgur is cooked through. Season with the remaining ½ teaspoon of salt, stirring well to incorporate.

Ladle into bowls and serve hot, topped with avocado and scallions, to taste.

CHIPOTLE POZOLE

MAKES 4 TO 6 SERVINGS

Call it a flash in the sheet pan; this quick version of the traditional Mexican stew gets its robust flavor from chipotle chiles, which are simply smoked jalapeños packed in a spicy tomato sauce. Creamy pinto beans and hominy corn mingle in a soothing yet spicy broth, accented by crisp fresh cabbage and radishes on top. Serve with tortilla chips on the side for a full-on fiesta!

POZOLE:

¼ cup olive oil
1 medium onion, diced
2 chipotles canned in adobo,
    chopped, plus 1 tablespoon adobo
    sauce, divided
2 teaspoons ground cumin
2 teaspoons smoked paprika
1 teaspoon ground coriander
½ teaspoon salt
½ teaspoon ground black pepper
2 (14.5-ounce) cans fire-roasted diced
    tomatoes
2–3 cups vegetable stock, divided
1 (28-ounce) can white hominy, rinsed
    and drained
1 (15-ounce) can (1½ cups cooked)
    pinto beans, rinsed and drained
1 bay leaf

TO SERVE:

1 cup green cabbage, finely shredded
1 cup fresh cilantro, roughly chopped
3–4 radishes, thinly sliced

Preheat your oven to 350°F and drizzle the oil all over a half sheet pan, tilting it around to thoroughly coat the bottom.

Add the onion along with the chipotles and place in the center of your oven. Cook until the onions are translucent, and the vegetables softened; about 5 to 8 minutes. Sprinkle in the cumin, paprika, coriander, salt, and pepper, stirring to combine. Return the sheet pan to the oven and let bake for another 2 minutes for the spices to release their full flavors.

Quickly add the diced tomatoes to prevent anything from burning, followed by the adobo sauce and about ½ cup of the vegetable stock. Incorporate the hominy, beans, and bay leaf next, stirring well.

Carefully move the sheet pan back into the oven and cook for 10 to 15 minutes, until the mixture is bubbling hot. Add more stock if needed to keep the mixture moist.

To serve, distribute the mixture between bowls and top off with the remaining vegetable stock and cabbage, cilantro, and radishes as desired.

FRENCH ONION SOUP

MAKES 4 SERVINGS

Rainy days call for endless bowlfuls of soup. Cold, wet, clammy, and seeking comfort, I won't even bother removing my jacket before banging a stock pot onto the stove. Soup is the only thing that can make the situation better; the simpler, the better. French onion is at the top of the list, rich and soothing, without any challenging preparation to contend with on a day that's already difficult to endure. A pinch of baking soda is the secret ingredient that speeds up the caramelization process, creating intensely flavored results in a fraction of the time. With a bare handful of pantry staples and a bit of restorative time in the kitchen, we can weather any storm.

3 pounds (about 6 medium) yellow onions, halved and sliced
3 cloves garlic, roughly chopped
¼ cup olive oil
1 tablespoon molasses
1 teaspoon dried thyme
½ teaspoon salt
¼ teaspoon ground black pepper
⅛ teaspoon baking soda
2 tablespoons dry white wine
1 tablespoon balsamic vinegar
1 tablespoon soy sauce
1 cup vegetable or mushroom stock

Preheat your oven to 350°F.

Combine the onions and garlic on a half sheet pan. Drizzle with the oil and molasses, sprinkle with thyme, salt, pepper, and baking soda, and toss everything together until evenly coated.

Cover the pan with foil and roast in the oven for 25 minutes, stirring once halfway through. The onions should start to look golden by now and be irresistibly aromatic. Remove the foil and carefully add the wine, vinegar, and soy sauce, mixing to incorporate. Continue to cook for an additional 35 to 45 minutes, stirring every 15 minutes, until caramelized to a deep mahogany brown.

Distribute the onion mixture equally between four bowls. Top each bowl with ¼ cup of vegetable stock and mix well before serving.

GARLICKY GREENS AND BEANS STEW

MAKES 6 SERVINGS

An ideal meal for taking the edge off a chilly fall or winter day, this simple stew is just the thing to warm your belly, nourish your mind, and sustain you through a full day of work. Any sort of beans will do in this simple mixture, so don't feel compelled to go out in search of a rare bean blend. Your best bets are bigger, meatier varieties, such as kidney beans, lima beans, fava beans, corona beans, or gigantes beans. Honestly though, any beans at all will do! If you don't have a bulk supply of cooked beans handy, you'll need two 14-ounce cans.

¼ cup olive oil
1 medium red onion, diced
1 whole bulb garlic (12–15 cloves),
    peeled and finely minced
8 ounces mushrooms, roughly
    chopped
1 dried bay leaf
1 teaspoon dried basil
1 teaspoon dried rosemary
2 teaspoons smoked paprika
½ teaspoon ground cumin
½ teaspoon ground coriander
¼ teaspoon red pepper flakes
2 tablespoons soy sauce
1 (28-ounce) can diced tomatoes
1 large (about 12 ounces) sweet
    potato, peeled and finely diced
3 cups cooked beans
1 large bunch (about 1 pound) kale,
    stems removed and roughly
    chopped
1 cup mushroom or vegetable stock
2 tablespoons balsamic vinegar
½ teaspoon salt
½ teaspoon ground black pepper

Preheat your oven to 350°F and drizzle the olive oil over a half sheet pan, coating the bottom thoroughly.

Spread the onion, garlic, and mushrooms out evenly over the prepared sheet and bake for 8 to 10 minutes, until softened and aromatic. Stir thoroughly and return the sheet to the oven for another 6 to 8 minutes, until the onion has lightly browned around the edges.

Add in the spices and seasonings, along with the tomatoes and sweet potato. Stir well, loosely cover with aluminum foil, and return the sheet to the oven. Cook for 20 to 25 minutes, until the potatoes are fork tender.

Uncover the sheet pan, add in the cooked beans and kale, scattering the leaves evenly over the top. Bake for a final 10 minutes or so, until the kale has wilted.

Carefully deglaze the pan with the stock, scraping the bottom with your spatula to incorporate all the caramelized goodies. Mix in the balsamic vinegar and season with salt and pepper. Serve hot, ideally with a chunk of crusty bread or over a bowlful of rice.

MINESTRONE PRIMAVERA

MAKES 6 SERVINGS

Minestrone is essentially the Swiss army knife of soups. It's an all-purpose tool for converting scraps foraged from the fridge into a respectable meal that never fails to delight. Though typically painted in deep shades of red, leaning heavily on slowly simmered tomatoes, this brothy beauty positively glows in a robe of spring finery. Golden beets, asparagus, and green peas feature prominently in this savory sea, flecked with feathery dill and sprightly fresh mint. Pasta is the only constant thread woven into every minestrone, lending heft to this bright ode to seasonal produce. Don't get stuck in a rut making the same soup all year round; the only limiting factor is your appetite!

¼ cup olive oil, divided
1 small leek, cleaned and sliced
1 small golden beet, peeled and diced
½ cup shredded carrots
2 stalks celery, diced
4 cloves garlic, minced
¾ teaspoon salt
½ pound asparagus, cut into 1-inch pieces
½ pound radishes, sliced
4 ounces pasta, such as elbows, small shells, ditalini, or orzo
6–7 cups vegetable stock, hot, divided
2 cups fresh spinach, roughly chopped
1½ cups frozen green peas, thawed
2 tablespoons lemon juice
2 tablespoons fresh mint, minced
2 tablespoons fresh dill, minced

Preheat your oven to 350°F and coat a half sheet pan with 2 tablespoons of olive oil. Add the sliced leek and golden beet, and roast for 15 minutes. The leek should be starting to brown around the edges. Add the shredded carrots, celery, and garlic right on top. Season with salt and cook for another 10 minutes, until the beets are fork tender and the whole mixture is highly aromatic.

Distribute the asparagus and radishes on top, and drizzle with the remaining 2 tablespoons of olive oil. Return everything to the oven for 5 to 10 minutes, until the asparagus is bright green.

Stir the vegetables thoroughly and add the pasta. Carefully pour in just enough stock to cover the pasta; 1 to 2 cups. Return the sheet to the oven and let cook for about 8 to 10 minutes, until the pasta is al dente, adding more stock as needed to keep everything moistened.

Remove the sheet from the oven and stir in the spinach, allowing it to wilt into the mixture from the residual heat. Stir in the peas, lemon juice, mint, and dill, making sure they're fully incorporated throughout.

Divide the vegetables and pasta equally between 6 bowls. Top off with hot vegetable stock, adding enough to make each portion appropriately soupy, based on your preference for how thick or thin you'd like it. Serve right away while piping hot.

The real beauty of minestrone is that it never goes out of season. Improvise using any fresh vegetable at their peak, no matter the time of year. In the summer, tomatoes, zucchini, corn, and green beans are essential. Come fall, finely diced cubes of butternut squash, fennel, broccoli florets, and shredded kale really hit the spot. Winter cries out for diced sweet potato, cauliflower, turnips, and parsnips, if you ask me. Mix and match at will, add and subtract to taste; there's no wrong way to build your bowl!

MUSHROOM BARLEY SOUP

MAKES 4 TO 6 SERVINGS

Matzo ball soup has the greatest claim to fame when it comes to Jewish stews and brews, but did you know that classic mushroom barley soup has the same storied heritage? Eastern European Jews knew that mushrooms were a rich source of flavor and nutrition long before the word "umami" had resonance beyond Japan. Foraging was essential for thrifty cooks trying to make ends meet, which is why the abundant fungi ended up in so many foundational recipes. From kugel to kreplach, it's the secret ingredient that simply tastes like home. No beef against western tradition, but there's simply no need for meat in this perfectly comforting classic.

3 tablespoons olive oil
1 medium yellow onion, diced
2 medium carrots, peeled and diced
1 pound sliced cremini or button
    mushrooms
4 cloves garlic, minced
½ teaspoon salt
¼ teaspoon ground black pepper
¾ cup dry pearl barley
6 cups vegetable stock, divided
2 tablespoons soy sauce
2 tablespoons balsamic vinegar
½ cup fresh parsley, minced

Preheat your oven to 350°F.

On a half sheet pan, toss together the oil, onions, carrots, mushrooms, and garlic. Season with salt and pepper, stirring thoroughly to combine. Bake in the center of the oven for about 10 minutes, until the vegetables are softened and fragrant.

Add the pearl barley followed by 3 cups of the vegetable stock, soy sauce, and balsamic vinegar. Cover the pan loosely with aluminum foil and cook for about 45 to 60 minutes, checking every 15 minutes or so, stirring thoroughly.

Once the barley is tender and the liquid is mostly absorbed, remove the pan from the oven and distribute the mixture between bowls. Top each bowl off with the remaining stock and fresh parsley, to serve.

PUMPKIN KHICHDI

MAKES 3 TO 4 SERVINGS

Khichdi, an Indian staple made of rice and lentils, is one of the simplest, genuinely healthy comfort foods that is guaranteed to cure what ails you. Soft, warm, and soothing, it's like the culinary equivalent of a weighted blanket, providing reassurance in times of sickness or strife. Far better than micro glass beads or plastic poly pellets, the contents of this essential stew are highly flexible, employing pantry goods that a well-stocked kitchen should always have in the first place. Pretty much any grain and bean will do; adjust the timing based on how long it takes to make both meltingly tender.

1 tablespoon coconut oil
½ teaspoon ground cumin
½ teaspoon ground ginger
½ jalapeño, seeded and minced
1 Roma tomato, diced
⅛ teaspoon ground turmeric
½ teaspoon salt
½ cup rice (or quinoa, steel cut oats, or millet)
½ cup red lentils (or moong dal, or split yellow peas)
½ cup pumpkin puree
3–4 cups water
Fresh cilantro, to serve

Preheat your oven to 350°F and set out a half sheet pan. Add the coconut oil and place it in the oven just long enough for it to melt.

Add the cumin, ginger, and jalapeño, toasting them in the oven for just about 1 to 2 minutes, until fragrant. Add the tomato, turmeric, and salt, stir well, and bake for another 2 minutes to soften. Sprinkle the rice and lentils evenly across the sheet pan.

Whisk together the pumpkin puree and water until smooth, then carefully pour it into the sheet pan, making sure it doesn't splash out. Stir gently to incorporate and cover lightly with aluminum foil. Bake for 50 to 60 minutes, stirring well after 30 minutes. Add another ½ cup of water if it begins looking dry before the grains and legumes are tender.

Pull the sheet out of the oven and stir vigorously to break down the contents, turning it into a chunky, creamy stew. Add another ½ cup of water to reach your desired consistency, if needed. Top with fresh cilantro to serve.

You can further dress this dish up by serving with unsweetened, plain vegan yogurt, pickles, relish, or chutney.

ROASTED TOMATO GAZPACHO

MAKES 3 TO 4 SERVINGS

Gazpacho is indeed a dish best served cold, but that doesn't mean it needs to be a raw deal. Adding fire roasted tomatoes is a quick shortcut to deeper, savory flavor, adding richness without the butter or cream associated with a long-simmered bisque. I like to make a big batch and keep it in a pitcher to drink down on hot days. Forget about green juices or smoothies; chilled vegetable soups are the coolest blends around!

2 tablespoons olive oil
2 pounds (4–6 medium) tomatoes, diced
½ medium red bell pepper, finely diced
½ medium red onion, finely diced
1 clove garlic, minced
1 (15-ounce) can tomato sauce
½ cup vegetable stock
2 tablespoons red wine vinegar
1 teaspoon horseradish or wasabi paste
2 teaspoons soy sauce
½ teaspoon salt
¼ teaspoon smoked paprika
¼ teaspoon ground black pepper
½ pound (2 small Persian or ½ English) seedless cucumbers, finely diced
2 tablespoons fresh basil, thinly sliced

Preheat your oven to 400°F. Drizzle the olive oil all over a half sheet pan, tilting the sheet to completely coat the bottom.

Add the tomatoes, pepper, onion, and garlic to the sheet pan, tossing to combine. Slide the sheet into the center of your oven and roast for 35 to 40 minutes, stirring thoroughly every 15 minutes or so, until the vegetables are tender, highly aromatic, and lightly charred around the edges. Let cool completely.

Transfer everything to a large pitcher and stir in the tomato sauce, vegetable stock, vinegar, horseradish, soy sauce, salt, paprika, pepper, and cucumber. Stir gently to combine.

Let the soup rest in the fridge for at least 1 to 3 hours, or until thoroughly chilled. The gazpacho can be prepared up to 1 day in advance if kept in an airtight container. Add fresh basil just before serving and enjoy cold.

ROASTED ZUCCHINI AND CHICKPEAS EN BRODO

MAKES 2 TO 4 SERVINGS

Gently crisped chickpeas give this soup a satisfying heft, while remaining light and refreshing due to the simple sea of broth surrounding them. Roasted zucchini is somehow greater than the sum of its parts, tender and sweet, singing of nature's bounty in every bite. Deeply comforting served either hot or chilled, I happen to adore it as a cooling foil to a scorching summer day.

1 medium yellow onion, diced

2 medium zucchini, quartered and diced

1 (15-ounce) can (1½ cups cooked) chickpeas, rinsed and drained

3 cloves garlic, minced

2 tablespoons avocado oil or olive oil

½ teaspoon salt

¼ teaspoon ground black pepper

2 cups vegetable stock

2 tablespoons fresh parsley, roughly chopped

Preheat your oven to 400°F and line a half sheet pan with aluminum foil or parchment paper. This makes for effortless clean-up; all you have to do is toss the foil or paper when you're all done, no washing required!

Arrange your chopped veggies, drained and rinsed chickpeas, and garlic on your prepared sheet pan in one even layer. Drizzle with oil and sprinkle with salt and pepper.

Slide everything into the oven and roast for 35 to 40 minutes, until the onions are just lightly browned and crispy around the edges, and the zucchini is tender. Let cool completely if you plan on serving the soup chilled.

Gently scoop the roasted veggies and chickpeas off the sheet and distribute them equally between bowls. Top off the vegetable stock, either warmed or chilled. Right before serving, finish with parsley.

RUBY BEET BORSCHT

MAKES 4 TO 6 SERVINGS

Call me an eighty-year-old Bubbeh at heart, but I love this old-world stew. It comes from the ancient Slavic word for beetroot, so it should come as no surprise that each ladleful dishes out an arresting crimson liquid that seems to smolder with bold flavor, despite its chilly temperature. That's the beauty of a proper borscht; a study in contrasts, each cold spoonful soothes and invigorates, calms and excites at the same time. Add a dollop of vegan sour cream if you must, but don't be alarmed if you end up with a hot pink hue staring back at you. For best results, pair it with a thick slice of rye bread to soak in every last drop.

2 tablespoons olive oil
6 small (1½ pounds) beets, peeled
  and diced
1 medium red onion, diced
2 medium carrots, peeled and diced
2 cloves garlic, minced
1 pound (½ small head) red cabbage,
  roughly chopped
1 (28-ounce) can petite diced
  tomatoes
2 tablespoons apple cider vinegar
4–6 cups hot vegetable stock, divided
1 teaspoon salt
½ teaspoon ground black pepper
¼ cup fresh dill, minced
Vegan sour cream or plain,
  unsweetened yogurt (optional)

Preheat your oven to 375°F. On a half sheet pan, toss together the olive oil, beets, red onion, carrots, garlic, and red cabbage. Arrange in a single layer and cover with aluminum foil. Place on the middle rack in your oven and roast until the beets and carrots are fork-tender; 30 to 45 minutes.

Remove the foil and stir in the tomatoes and vinegar. Increase the heat to 400°F and cook for another 8 to 10 minutes, until the edges of the cabbage begin to get caramelized and crispy.

Remove the sheet pan from the oven. Deglaze with 1 cup of vegetable stock, stirring thoroughly and scraping the bottom of the pan with your spatula to incorporate all the delicious browned bits of vegetables. Add the salt, pepper, and dill, stirring to incorporate.

Divide the vegetable mixture between bowls and top off with stock to reach your desired consistency. Garnish with vegan sour cream or yogurt if you'd like to add a cool, creamy finish.

> **On hot days, this soup is brilliantly refreshing if served chilled. As another way to switch things up, it's wonderful blended to either a chunky or completely smooth bisque.**

YAKI UDON NOODLE SOUP

MAKES 3 TO 4 SERVINGS

Take the delightful wok-kissed char of yaki udon and combine it with the soothing properties of shoyu ramen, all without putting a single pot on the stove. It tastes like some sort of black magic, but it's merely your resident sheet pan, hard at work. Scorching the starchy strands before applying broth gives them a crisp, satisfying caramelized edge while retaining their characteristically chewy texture within. When you can't decide between stir fry and soup, this is the perfect compromise that makes no concessions.

3 tablespoons olive oil, divided
8 ounces extra-firm tofu, thoroughly
    drained
1 pound fresh udon noodles
½ medium yellow onion, sliced
¼ medium head green cabbage,
    shredded
1 cup fresh shiitake mushrooms, sliced
1 cup shredded carrots
3 tablespoons soy sauce
2 tablespoons mirin or cooking sherry
2 scallions, thinly sliced
2–3 cups hot mushroom or vegetable
    stock

Preheat your oven to 400°F. Drizzle 1 tablespoon of the oil over a half sheet pan, tilting it around to thoroughly coat the bottom.

Cut the tofu in half lengthwise. Slice into ½-inch-thick rectangles and lay them out without overlapping on one side of the sheet pan. Bake on the top rack of the oven for 15 minutes.

Remove the sheet from the oven and flip the tofu to the opposite side. Rinse the noodles under warm water to gently separate. Spread them out to cover the empty side of the sheet pan. Drizzle with 1 tablespoon of oil, toss with the onion, and return the pan to the oven.

Bake for another 15 minutes and stir thoroughly, adding the cabbage, mushrooms, and carrots. Mix everything together and drizzle with the remaining tablespoon of oil, soy sauce, and mirin.

Bake for a final 15 to 20 minutes, until the tofu is crispy, the noodles are lightly charred, and the vegetables are tender. Add the scallions, tossing to incorporate.

Divide the mixture equally between four bowls. Top them off with enough vegetable stock to submerge all the goodies. Enjoy right away, while hot!

> **If you'd prefer a dry stir fry, just omit the stock and you'll have a beautifully charred noodle dish that you'd swear was just kissed by the heat of a blazing steel wok.**

ENTREES

BBQ BAKED BEAN LOADED POTATOES

MAKES 4 SERVINGS

Baked potatoes were the foundation of my diet when I first went vegan and in fact, were my first consciously vegan meal. Sitting in a squeaky plastic booth at local greasy spoon diner with my family many years ago, I was ready to prove a point and commit to the effort, full stop. Perhaps it could have been better planned because I was relegated to one single option sans meat, dairy, and eggs: a plain, steamed baked potato, with two little packets of salt and pepper on the side. That didn't dampen my love for spuds nor dissuade me from taking the cruelty-free path. If anything, it was the catalyst for greater culinary creativity, stemming from humble beginnings.

Endlessly adaptable, versatile, and accommodating, absolutely everything goes well with potatoes. Many early meals consisted of a hot and fluffy potato doused in prepared, canned chili. I've stepped up my game considerably since them, preferring the more nuanced smoky blend of tender beans bathed in barbeque sauce, slowly baked to concentrate their sweetness. Tempeh bacon contributes a convincingly meaty bite to win over omnivores and satisfy herbivores alike. There's nothing wrong with a simple spud every now and then, but if you're trying to convert a reluctant eater, you'll have much better luck with this fully loaded, flavor-packed approach.

BAKED POTATOES:
- 2 large russet or sweet potatoes
- 1 tablespoon olive oil

TEMPEH BACON:
- 3 tablespoons soy sauce
- 1 tablespoon maple syrup
- 1 tablespoon olive oil
- 1 teaspoon apple cider vinegar
- ½ teaspoon liquid smoke
- ¼ teaspoon ground paprika
- 1 (8-ounce) package tempeh, thinly sliced

BBQ BAKED BEANS:
- 2 (14-ounce) cans (3 cups cooked) white beans or pinto beans
- 1 cup barbeque sauce, divided
- 1 teaspoon instant coffee powder
- 1 teaspoon apple cider vinegar

TO SERVE:
- 2 scallions, thinly sliced

Preheat your oven to 400°F. Line a half sheet pan with parchment paper or a silicon baking mat.

Rub down the potatoes with olive oil, thoroughly and completely coating the outsides. Cut a slit down the center of each with a sharp knife and place them one end of your prepared sheet pan. The potatoes will take longest, so get them baking first. Give them a 15-minute head start while you prepare the tempeh bacon.

In a small dish, whisk together the soy sauce, maple syrup, olive oil, apple cider vinegar, liquid smoke, and paprika. Layer in the sliced tempeh, gently tossing to coat. Let marinate during the first 15 minutes while the potatoes get started.

Carefully remove the sheet pan from the oven and lay out the tempeh strips in an even layer, lined up next to the potatoes, leaving the far end of the sheet empty. Return everything to the oven and bake for another 15 minutes.

(Continued on next page)

Meanwhile, combine the beans, ½ cup of the barbeque sauce, instant coffee, and apple cider vinegar in a small bowl.

After a total of 30 minutes have elapsed, flip the tempeh and add the beans on the remaining open space on the sheet pan. Bake for another 10 minutes and stir the remaining ½ cup of barbeque sauce into the beans. Give it just 5 more minutes to warm through, making for a total of 45 minutes of baking time, and remove the sheet from the oven. Let stand for 15 minutes, or until the tempeh is cool enough to handle.

Crumble or roughly chop the tempeh into small pieces to mimic bacon bits. Split potatoes in half and fluff the insides with a fork.

For each serving, place one potato half on a plate and top with ¼ of the beans and ¼ of the crumbled tempeh. Finish with a sprinkle of sliced scallions on top.

Feel free to lavish your potatoes with shredded vegan cheese, a dollop of sour cream, diced avocado, fresh cilantro, or any of your other favorite toppings if you want to go all-out!

CHAKALAKA

MAKES 6 TO 10 SERVINGS

Boom chakalaka—this South African dish is a slam dunk! It's almost as satisfying to say as it is to eat. The etymology of the word "chakalaka" comes from the Zulu language, meaning "all together," but its history is a bit elusive. Said to have originated from Johannesburg, where gold miners cooked canned beans and tomatoes with whatever fresh vegetables they had available, spicing it generously to combat the midday heat. Varying from mild to excruciatingly hot, there's no one formula for success; every family has their own special chakalaka recipe, and of course, everyone's own approach is the best one.

Versatile to the point of being almost impossible to define, it fits into many categories, depending on who's doing the cooking. Some prepare it finely chopped and chilled, as a salsa or relish, while others soup it up to serve as a satisfyingly spicy stew. My preference is a drier preparation, mixed with white beans to create a balanced, complete meal all at once. The only mandatory components are bell peppers and tomatoes, but it's not uncommon to find anything from cauliflower to shredded cabbage added into the mix. Don't be afraid to improvise with anything else you have on hand.

CHAKALAKA:
2 tablespoons olive oil
1 tablespoon maple syrup
2 cloves garlic, sliced
2 tablespoons mild yellow curry powder (such as madras)
1½ teaspoons ground ginger
½ teaspoon dried thyme
¾ teaspoon salt
¼ teaspoon ground black pepper
1 medium yellow onion, halved and sliced
1 red bell pepper, seeded and sliced
1 yellow bell pepper, seeded and sliced
1 orange bell pepper, seeded and sliced
2–3 jalapeños, seeded and diced
1 cup baby carrots
4 Roma tomatoes, sliced into wedges
1 (14-ounce) can white beans, drained

TO SERVE:
Cooked white or brown rice (optional)

Preheat your oven to 375°F and set out 2 nonstick half sheet pans.

In a large bowl, combine the oil, maple syrup, garlic, curry powder, ginger, thyme, salt, and pepper. Add in the onion, all three peppers, jalapeño, and baby carrots. Toss to coat before spreading the goods out equally between the two prepared pans. Roast for 25 minutes, stirring about halfway through, until lightly toasted around the edges.

Carefully open the oven, rotate the sheets, and add the tomatoes and beans, distributing them equally. Stir well to incorporate. Continue to cook for 15 minutes longer, until the peppers are blistered, tomatoes are meltingly tender, and the beans are warmed through.

Serve alongside hot cooked rice, if desired.

CHICKPEA PAN PIE

MAKES 6 TO 8 SERVINGS

May we all be so fortunate to have a chickpea in every pot pie. Cradled in a flaky, golden crust, chickpeas and green peas commingle with the classic French mirepoix of onion, carrots, celery, and savory spices. Uniquely suited to the sheet pan format, you ensure that everyone gets a fair piece of this pie, with generous amounts of that beautifully buttery crust to go around. Plus, you don't even need to make the pastry from scratch, making this feast an effortless quick fix any day of the week. Creamy without being heavy, this is one hearty meal that still won't weigh you down.

2 tablespoons olive oil

1 small yellow onion, diced

2 carrots, peeled and diced

3 stalks celery, diced

½ teaspoon salt

½ teaspoon ground black pepper

2 cups vegetable stock

1 tablespoon soy sauce

¼ cup chickpea flour

½ teaspoon dried thyme

½ teaspoon dried rosemary

2 (15-ounce) cans (3 cups cooked) chickpeas, drained

1 cup green peas, fresh or frozen and thawed

1 sheet (half of a 17.3-ounce package) puff pastry, thawed

Preheat oven to 400°F. Coat the bottom of a half sheet pan with olive oil and distribute the diced onion, carrots, and celery on top. Season with salt and pepper and roast for 14 to 16 minutes, stirring about halfway through, until golden, aromatic, and tender.

Meanwhile, whisk together the vegetable stock, soy sauce, chickpea flour, thyme, and rosemary. Make sure there are no lumps before pouring evenly all over the cooked vegetables. Add the chickpeas and green peas, stirring well to incorporate and distribute throughout the mixture.

On a lightly floured surface, roll the puff pastry out into a large rectangle approximately the same size as your sheet pan. Cut the dough into ½-inch-wide strips. Arrange the strips in a lattice pattern on top of filling, trimming to fit and pressing down gently to seal.

Alternately, use a cookie cutter to punch out any shapes your heart desires, and place them decoratively on top of the filling.

Return the sheet pan to the oven and bake until the pastry is golden brown, and the filling is thick and bubbly; about 20 to 25 minutes.

> **Want to put your prep on warp speed?** You can find mirepoix mixes already chopped and ready to go in the refrigerated section of the fresh produce area.

CHICKPEA TIKKA MASALA

MAKES 4 TO 6 SERVINGS

Redolent of warm spices and an undeniably savory scent, tikka masala lives and dies by its sauce. Chicken is the typical protein du jour, but in an exquisitely crafted curry, genuinely anything can seamlessly blend in. Chickpeas are a staple of Indian cuisine themselves, so it's not a stretch to trade the meat for beans. Initially sweet but switching over to spicy in seconds, the experience is invigorating and soothing in equal measure.

CHICKPEA TIKKA MASALA:
2 tablespoons olive oil
1 medium head cauliflower, cut into florets
1 red bell pepper, diced
1 (28-ounce can) diced tomatoes
2 cans chickpeas, drained
2 inches fresh ginger, peeled and finely minced
4 cloves garlic, minced
1 jalapeño, seeded and minced
½ cup full-fat coconut milk
2 tablespoons lime juice
1 teaspoon ground cumin
1 teaspoon smoked paprika
1 teaspoon garam masala
1 teaspoon salt
½ teaspoon ground turmeric
¼ teaspoon cayenne pepper

CUCUMBER RAITA:
1 cup plain, unsweetened vegan yogurt
½ seedless cucumber, finely shredded (about 1 cup)
1 clove garlic, finely minced
2 tablespoons fresh cilantro
½ teaspoon ground cumin
¼ teaspoon salt

TO SERVE:
¼ cup fresh cilantro, optional
Lime wedges

Preheat your oven to 400°F. Line two half-sheet pans with aluminum foil and coat each with 1 tablespoon of oil. Add the cauliflower and bell pepper, dividing them equally between the two pans, and toss together with your hands until lightly coated in oil.

Slide the sheets into your oven and roast for 20 minutes, until lightly browned.

Meanwhile, in a large bowl, combine the diced tomatoes, chickpeas, ginger, garlic, and jalapeño. In a separate bowl, combine the coconut milk, lime juice, cumin, paprika, garam masala, salt, turmeric, and cayenne. Make sure everything is thoroughly blended, with no lumps of dry spices remaining.

Open the oven door and carefully add in the tomato and chickpea mixture across both pans. Reduce the heat to 375°F and cook for another 10 minutes.

Add the liquid spice mixture and toss thoroughly to incorporated and make sure all the vegetables are cooking evenly, and bake for, 10 to 15 minutes longer; 40 to 45 minutes of cooking time in all.

When the entree reaches the final 10 minutes of cook time, go ahead and prepare the raita. Simply place all the ingredients in a bowl and mix until thoroughly combined. This can also be prepared up to a day in advance. Simply store it in the fridge in an airtight container. In either case, keep the raita chilled until dinnertime.

To serve, give the main dish a final stir, combining both sheets if desired for better consistency of seasoning. Spoon into bowls and top with fresh cilantro, and fresh lime wedges and raita on the side. Enjoy hot.

Stay cool as a cucumber and don't let those Cucurbitaceae water down your dish! For this application, I like to use an "extra coarse" microplane or fine box grater to get very thin slivers to start with. Then, I'll give them a firm squeeze over the sink to release some of the extra moisture. There's no need to salt or let the shreds sit; just apply some good old-fashioned manual pressure, and they should release plenty of cucumber juice. If you hate waste as much as I do, squeeze it over a glass, mix in some chilled soda water, and treat yourself to a refreshing drink!

DENGAKU DONBURI

MAKES 2 SERVINGS

Eggplant can be a fickle dinner guest. Stubbornly refusing to tenderize even under threat of torture, it remains staunchly uncooked, squeaky against the teeth, until completely collapsing into a mushy morass in the blink of an eye. Don't worry—it's not you, it's the eggplant.

Proper cookery is the key to coaxing the absolute best texture out of this mercurial ingredient. Sweet and salty miso sauce tenderizes meaty slices of eggplant to begin softening the flesh before it ever sees the heat of the oven. Then, primed for the spotlight, that same marinade thickens into a caramelized top layer, seeping into every open pore.

If eggplants still aren't on your list of invites, try the same technique with portobello mushrooms, slabs of extra-firm tofu, sliced zucchini, or rounds of daikon radish.

NASU DENGAKU:

2 medium Japanese or 1 Italian eggplant
½ pound firm tofu
¼ cup chickpea or white miso paste
2 tablespoons low-sodium soy sauce
2 tablespoons mirin
2 tablespoons rice vinegar
2 tablespoons maple syrup
1 teaspoon ground ginger
1 tablespoon toasted sesame seeds
1 scallion, thinly sliced

TO SERVE:

1–2 cups cooked sushi rice (optional)

Preheat your oven to 400°F and line a half sheet pan with parchment paper or a silicone baking mat.

Remove the calyx (the cap on top) from the eggplant(s) and slice into approximately ¼-inch-thick rounds. Arrange the pieces in a single layer on the sheet pan. Don't be afraid to break out a second pan if it won't all fit; there's a lot of variation in eggplant sizes. Slice the tofu into ¼-inch-thick rectangular slabs and lay out the pieces alongside the eggplant.

Bake for 20 minutes, flip all the vegetables and proteins, and bake for another 10 minutes.

Meanwhile, whisk together the miso paste, soy sauce, mirin, vinegar, maple syrup, and ginger in a medium bowl, creating an amber sauce, about the viscosity of pancake batter.

Remove the sheet pan from the oven and switch on the broiler to high. Spoon the sauce generously over all the eggplant and tofu pieces, allowing a substantial layer to pool on top of each one.

Broil on high for 8 to 10 minutes, until the sauce is no longer glossy and has softly set.

Sprinkle with sesame seeds and sliced scallion, and serve over warm sushi rice, if desired.

DIRTY RICED CAULIFLOWER

MAKES 4 TO 6 SERVINGS

Clean up your act with this riff on standard dirty rice by replacing grains with finely chopped cauliflower. Singing with bright spices and bursting with fresh flavor in every bite, you'd never even realize you just doubled your vegetable intake with one modest serving. Umami mushrooms add meatiness instead of conventional livers and gizzards, creating a "dirty" color without leaving blood on your hands.

2 tablespoons olive oil, divided

1 (8-ounce) package tempeh, roughly crumbled

4 ounces baby bella or button mushrooms, minced

1 medium yellow onion, finely chopped

2 stalks celery, diced

1 jalapeño pepper, seeded and finely chopped

1 teaspoon salt, divided

½ cup mushroom or vegetable stock

4 cups riced cauliflower

1½ teaspoons Cajun seasoning

½ teaspoon dried thyme

Preheat your oven to 375°F and coat the bottom of a half sheet pan with 1 tablespoon of the oil.

Spread the crumbled tempeh out on top in an even layer and bake for 15 minutes, until lightly browned around the edges. Add the minced mushrooms, onions, celery, and jalapeño, stirring well to incorporate. Season with half of the salt before sliding the mixture into the oven. Roast for another 15 minutes, until the vegetables are softened and aromatic, stirring halfway though.

Carefully deglaze by pouring in vegetable broth, scraping the bottom of the pan thoroughly with your spatula to dislodge any pieces that might have stuck, preventing them from burning.

Add the riced cauliflower right on top, along with the Cajun seasoning, thyme, and remaining salt. Drizzle with the rest of the oil and stir well to incorporate, distributing the vegetables throughout.

Cook for 5 to 10 minutes longer, until the cauliflower is tender, and the liquid has largely evaporated. Serve hot, or let cool, chill thoroughly, and enjoy as a cold salad later.

EGGPLANT SHAWARMA

MAKES 4 SERVINGS

Spinning in an endless loop over an open flame, highly aromatic spices fill the air as shawarma roasts, proteins slowly caramelizing until the exterior is shaved away in paper-thin sheets, only to begin the browning process anew. You can smell it from a mile away, beckoning with the heady aroma of cumin, paprika, coriander, ginger, cardamom, and more.

Bathed in this rich olfaction ocean, eggplant glistens under the glow of hot oven coils, considerably simplifying the time-honored practice. It's a potent meal-starter for any occasion; ideal as sandwich fodder, hummus-topper, or rice bowl feature, my favorite serving suggestion employs the classic pita wrap. Cool, fresh vegetables and tangy yogurt sauce contrast the warm filling, swaddled in soft, fluffy flatbread. Wrap it in foil to take it to go or dig right in immediately. The temptation to eat right off the sheet pan isn't the worst to give into, either.

EGGPLANT SHAWARMA:

- 1 medium (¾–1 pound) globe eggplant
- 3 tablespoons olive oil
- 2 teaspoons ground cumin
- 1 teaspoon smoked paprika
- ¾ teaspoon ground coriander
- ¼ teaspoon ground ginger
- ¼ teaspoon cardamom
- ⅛ teaspoon cayenne pepper
- ½ teaspoon salt

TO SERVE:

- 4 pitas or flatbread
- ½ small red onion, thinly sliced
- 2 Roma tomatoes, thinly sliced
- 2 cups shredded romaine lettuce
- ½ cup plain, unsweetened vegan yogurt
- 2 cloves garlic, minced
- ½ teaspoon ground black pepper

Preheat your oven to 400°F and line a half sheet pan with parchment paper or a silicone baking mat.

Cut off the calyx on the eggplant and slice it into ¼-inch-thick rounds. Cut the rounds into 1-inch-wide strips and place them in a large bowl along with the oil. Sprinkle in all the spices and salt, gently stirring to coat the eggplant evenly.

Spread the strips out in a single layer on your prepared baking sheet, and roast for 20 to 30 minutes, until tender and lightly caramelized around the edges. Let cool for at least 5 minutes.

To serve, you can either stuff the pita pockets or use them as flatbread, layering the accoutrement on top. In any event, build your meal with the pita as a base, and add sliced red onion, tomatoes, lettuce, and warm eggplant as desired. Whisk together the yogurt, garlic, and pepper in a small dish before drizzling liberally all over everything. Wrap it all up and roll out!

GENERAL TSO'S TOFU

MAKES 3 TO 4 SERVINGS

General Tso may or may not have been a real person, but the dish that bears his name is unarguably a takeout staple that transcends traditional culinary boundaries. The trouble is, the meat of the matter is usually of the lowest quality, deep fried, and though delicious, difficult to rationalize as a regular dinner selection. Put away the menus and turn on the oven for a far healthier approach that takes hardly any effort. The entire meal is built on a single sheet pan, making both prep and cleanup a breeze. Even the general himself would be impressed.

1 (14-ounce) package extra-firm tofu, drained
¼ cup tapioca starch
1½ teaspoons garlic powder
1½ teaspoons ground ginger
1 tablespoon toasted sesame oil, divided
⅓ cup vegetable stock
3 tablespoons soy sauce
2 tablespoons rice vinegar
2 tablespoons water
1 tablespoon tomato sauce
1 tablespoon coconut sugar or dark brown sugar, firmly packed
1 teaspoon sriracha
2 cups broccoli florets
Steamed white rice, to serve (optional)

Preheat your oven 425°F and lightly grease a half sheet pan.

Slice the tofu crosswise into ½-inch slabs and cut each of those on the diagonal to make neat little triangles. Layer the tofu pieces in a clean, absorbent dish towel and set something heavy (like a skillet with a can or two of beans) on top to press out as much of the excess water as possible. Allow 15 to 20 minutes before proceeding.

In a shallow bowl, whisk together the tapioca starch, garlic powder, and ginger. Unwrap the tofu and toss it in the dry mixture, shaking off but reserving the excess. Transfer the pieces to your prepared baking sheet without any of them overlapping and drizzle with half of the sesame oil. Bake for 30 minutes.

Meanwhile, take the leftover starch mixture and whisk in the remaining oil, along with the vegetable stock, soy sauce, vinegar, water, tomato sauce, sugar, and sriracha.

At the 30-minute mark, add the broccoli onto the sheet pan and pour the sauce all over the tofu and vegetables. Bake for another 5 to 10 minutes, stirring every 5 minutes to prevent anything from sticking and burning on the bottom of the pan, until the broccoli is bright green, and the sauce has thickened to a glossy consistency. Serve alongside steamed rice, if desired.

Drawing inspiration from early autumnal bounty, it's truly a feast fit for a celebration. The real beauty is that it's infinitely adaptable, able to accommodate anything that Mother Nature has to offer. Swap out the apple for a pear or even fresh apricots; use yellow squash or pattypan squash instead of zucchini; try delicata or a small sugar pumpkin to replace the kabocha (but peel the pumpkin first, please!); trade out carrots for parsnips, yams, potatoes, or turnips.

HARVEST TAGINE

MAKES 10 TO 12 SERVINGS

Okay, you got me: a tagine is a specific cooking vessel, not the name of a dish by itself. Over time and misuse, however, it's become synonymous with the classic preparation of rich Moroccan spices, vegetables, and fluffy couscous. Allow me the poetic liberty of applying that moniker here to a simpler version, made without the earthen clay pot.

Laden with slow-roasted squash, root vegetables, and caramelized onions, the multicolored mélange of produce is just the beginning. Dig deeper to uncover a warmly spiced chickpea curry, freckled with fresh herbs, and punctuated with briny capers and plump, sweet raisins. Explore further still, and eventually your spoon will hit gold; a vibrant bed of garlicky, flaxen couscous lovingly cradles the savory mountain with ease.

HARVEST TAGINE:

- 1 tart green apple, peeled, cored, and sliced
- ½ large red onion, quartered and sliced
- 1 medium zucchini, sliced
- 1 small (about 1¾–2 pounds) kabocha squash, halved, seeded, and sliced
- 1 cup baby carrots
- 4 tablespoons olive oil, divided
- 1 teaspoon salt
- 4 cloves garlic, minced
- 2 teaspoons smoked paprika
- 1¼ teaspoons ground cumin
- 1 teaspoon ground coriander
- 1 teaspoon ground ginger
- ¼ teaspoon ground cinnamon
- ⅛ teaspoon saffron, crushed
- ¼ teaspoon crushed red pepper flakes
- 1 (14-ounce) can (1¾ cups cooked) chickpeas, drained
- ¼ cup raisins
- ¼ cup capers, drained
- 3 tablespoons lemon juice
- 3 tablespoons tomato paste
- ½ cup water
- ½ cup fresh parsley, roughly chopped
- ¼ cup toasted pine nuts

GOLDEN COUSCOUS:

- 2 tablespoons olive oil
- 2 cloves garlic, minced
- 2¼ cups vegetable stock
- ½ teaspoon ground turmeric
- 10 ounces (1½ cups) dry couscous

Preheat your oven to 400°F and lightly grease 2 half sheet pans.

Begin by breaking down all the apple, onion, zucchini, and kabocha squash, and laying them out on the prepared sheet pans, along with the baby carrots, in one even layer. Drizzle evenly with 2 tablespoons of the olive oil, and sprinkle evenly with salt. Roast for 30 minutes, rotating the pans about halfway through. The vegetables won't be quite done yet but beginning to soften and brown nicely. There's no need to flip or stir as long as you adjust the sheets on higher and lower levels as you spin them around.

Meanwhile, in a medium bowl, whisk together remaining oil, minced garlic, all the spices, chickpeas, raisins, capers, lemon juice, tomato paste, and water. It should look sort of like a chunky bean soup.

Pour this liquid seasoning mixture all over the vegetables, distributing it as evenly as possible between the two sheets. Stir thoroughly but gently to incorporate, being careful to scrape up any caramelized bits on the bottom of the pans. Continue baking for 20 to 30 minutes longer, until evenly browned and fork-tender.

(Continued on next page)

For the couscous, keep a close eye on the clock. After the vegetables have been cooking for about 45 minutes all told, place a quarter sheet pan in the oven and coat the bottom with oil. Scatter the minced garlic on top, and toast for 2 minutes. Whisk together the stock and turmeric, and carefully pour it in. Allow 5 minutes for it the liquid to warm before sprinkling in the dry couscous. Stir well to thoroughly moisten and leave the pan in the oven for just 1 minute longer. Remove the sheet, cover tightly with foil, and let it steam for 5 minutes, undisturbed.

When ready to serve, fluff the couscous with a fork before transferring it to the bottom of a large ceramic tagine, platter, or bowl. Top with the vegetable and bean mixture, sprinkle with parsley and pine nuts, and present to your adoring audience, with or without great fanfare.

As a grand feast suitable for a holiday meal like Thanksgiving, the full affair might be intimidating to whip up on a whim, especially if space and time in the kitchen is limited. If you'd like to prepare the tagine in advance, you can make the entire assembly up to 5 hours before serving. Cover and store in the fridge. Reheat in an oven preheated to 375°F for 15 to 30 minutes, depending on how conductive your serving dish is. Just check periodically to see if it's hot all the way through.

You can also create the individual components up to 2 days in advance. Just store them separately in airtight containers in the fridge. Be sure to re-fluff the couscous before proceeding with the rest of the construction.

HUNGRY, HUNGRY HIPPIE PANINI

MAKES 6 SERVINGS

Living indefinitely on every cafe menu, it may not be designated so blatantly, but the hippie sandwich is a staple that many old school vegans gravitate towards. Harkening back to the simpler days before realistic plant-based meats or fancy flourishes, the focus is squarely placed on hearty whole wheat bread, cradling a cornucopia of fresh vegetables. Converting that concept to sheet pan cookery, you can create enough sandwiches to feed a whole commune of starving artists with this timeless, comforting combo.

12 slices whole wheat or multigrain
   sandwich bread
¼ cup olive oil, divided
¾ cup vegan cream cheese or
   hummus
1½ cups shredded carrots
1 (12-ounce jar) roasted red peppers,
   thoroughly drained
1½ cups fresh baby spinach, arugula,
   or sprouts, roughly chopped
3 medium avocados, sliced

Preheat your oven to 400°F.

Brush one side of 6 slices of bread with 1 teaspoon of oil each. Place the bread with the oiled side down on a half sheet pan. Top each with 2 tablespoons of cream cheese or hummus, ¼ cup of shredded carrots, enough red pepper to cover, ¼ cup of spinach, and ½ of an avocado.

Brush the remaining 6 slices of bread with 1 teaspoon of oil each, placing them on top of each stack with the oiled side facing up. Cover with another half sheet pan, weighing it down with a heavy cast iron skillet.

Carefully move the whole assembly into the center of your oven and bake 20 minutes. Remove skillet and top sheet pan and bake for a final 5 to 10 minutes until bread is golden brown, crisp, and evenly toasted.

Cut each sandwich in half to serve.

JERK SEITAN WITH TOSTONES

MAKES 2 TO 3 SERVINGS

Escape to the islands with a departure from your average weekday dinner. Smashed plantains, otherwise known as tostones, are poised to be the next French fry. Don't mistake them for bananas; they may look similar to the #1 bestselling fruit in America, but have a starchy profile more like the humble potato. Baked until tender and then smashed flat to achieve crispy, golden-brown edges, they're addictive as a snack all by themselves. Paired with the invigorating blend of tangy, spicy, sweet, and smoky flavors of jerk seitan, this meal will put you in an island state of mind, no matter where or when you choose to dig in.

JERK SEITAN:

3 tablespoons orange juice
2 tablespoons dark brown
    sugar, firmly packed
2 tablespoons soy sauce
1 tablespoon white vinegar
1 teaspoon ground ginger
½ teaspoon garlic powder
½ teaspoon dried thyme
¼ teaspoon ground
    cinnamon
¼ teaspoon ground allspice
½ habanero pepper, seeded
    and finely minced
10–12 ounces seitan, roughly
    chopped or shredded
1 scallion, thinly sliced

TOSTONES:

2 medium plantains
1 tablespoon coconut oil,
    melted
¼ teaspoon salt

Begin by preparing the jerk sauce, which comes together very quickly. Simply whisk together the orange juice, brown sugar, soy sauce, vinegar, ginger, garlic powder, thyme, cinnamon, allspice, and minced habanero in a medium bowl. Once smooth, add in the seitan and toss to coat. Set aside and let marinate for about 20 minutes, tossing again halfway through to make sure all the pieces get even coverage.

Meanwhile, preheat your oven to 425°F and line a half sheet pan with parchment paper or a silicone baking mat.

Peel the plantains by chopping off the ends with a sharp knife, and then making a shallow cut lengthwise just through the peel, not the fruit itself. Insert your thumb into the slit and gently coax the peel off the plantain.

Slice each plantain into ½-inch coins and spread them out on half of the prepared sheet pan, allowing a bit of space between each piece. Drizzle with coconut oil and sprinkle evenly with salt.

Spoon the marinated seitan out onto the opposite side of the sheet pan, straining out but reserving the excess jerk sauce.

Bake for 10 minutes, until the plantains begin to look a bit brown and dry around the edges. Remove the sheet, flip the plantains, and use the bottom of a flat measuring cup, jar, or drinking glass to press them out flat, smashing them down as thin as possible.

Drizzle half of the remaining marinade over the seitan before returning the pan to the oven. Bake for an additional 10 to 15 minutes, until the plantains are golden-brown and the seitan is crisp around the edges. Let cool before dividing between plates and topping the seitan with sliced scallions. Feel free to serve with hot sauce or spicy chutney if desired but make no mistake: this jerk is already packing some serious heat!

KABOCHA GNOCCHI WITH MISO BROWNED BUTTER

MAKES 4 TO 5 SERVINGS

Also known as beurre noisette in French, the direct translation of "hazelnut butter" is a far more elegant way of describing this rich nectar. Alluding to the toasty, hazelnut-like flavor derived from a quick flash in the pan, the application of gentle heat transforms everyday cooking fat into an otherworldly substance, redolent with complex savory notes that heighten the inherent umami of an ingredient lucky enough to anointed. Obstinate, old-school chefs would have you believe that this decadent liquid gold can only be made with dairy, but au contraire, I've found that the same process works just as well with vegan butter. Better yet, it caramelizes faster in a sheet pan with more direct contact to the hot surface, quickly going to work searing pillows of potato gnocchi and mellow Japanese pumpkin. Autumnal sage becomes shatteringly crisp in the process, perfuming the whole dish with an earthy aroma. Pecans add the final crunchy bite, but if you'd like to further the theme, chopped hazelnuts would be a natural match.

½ cup vegan butter
1 small kabocha squash (about 2 pounds), seeded and sliced into ½-inch wedges
1 yellow onion, halved and sliced
1 (14–16-ounce) package potato gnocchi
3 cloves garlic, minced
25–30 leaves fresh sage
⅛ teaspoon ground nutmeg
½ cup raw pecan halves
3 tablespoons chickpea miso
2 tablespoons lemon juice

Preheat your oven to 375°F.

Place the vegan butter right on a half sheet pan and slide it into the oven to melt. After about 5 minutes, it should have liquefied and started foaming lightly around the edges. Use an oven mitt to tilt the sheet pan around carefully, gently coating the bottom with melted butter.

Arrange the kabocha wedges on the sheet pan without overlapping, weaving the onion pieces in between. Bake for 10 minutes, until the onion is translucent and aromatic.

Remove the sheet from the oven and add the gnocchi, spreading them out so they have as much contact with the bottom of the pan as possible. Sprinkle evenly with the minced garlic, whole sage leaves, and nutmeg.

Bake for an additional 20 minutes, until the kabocha is fork-tender and lightly browned around the edges. Add the pecans on top and bake for just 5 minutes longer to toast the nuts. Let cool for 5 minutes.

Meanwhile, whisk together the miso paste and lemon juice in a small dish until smooth. Pour the mixture evenly all over the gnocchi and vegetables, gently tossing to coat. Distribute between plates and serve hot.

LAVASH LASAGNA

MAKES 6 TO 8 SERVINGS

Defined by its multitude of savory layers, the most impressive lasagnas are usually stacked up tall, towering over dinner plates like edible high rises. Though these culinary construction projects are awe-inspiring, it's not the height of the meal that matters, but the flavor. Take a page from flatbread, laid out with savory strata of remarkably cheesy tofu ricotta and rich tomato sauce. By skipping the noodles, there's no need to boil, and no fussy patchwork procedure to cover the full pan.

TOFU RICOTTA:

1 pound extra-firm tofu, thoroughly
   drained
¼ cup fresh basil, minced
2 tablespoons lemon juice
2 tablespoons nutritional yeast
1 tablespoon white miso paste
1 tablespoon olive oil
1 teaspoon onion powder
½ teaspoon garlic powder
½ teaspoon salt

TO ASSEMBLE:

3 cups (one 25-ounce jar) marinara
   sauce
4–5 (one 10-ounce package) sheets
   lavash flatbread

Preheat your oven to 350°F and lightly grease a half sheet pan.

Begin by preparing the tofu ricotta. Roughly crumble the tofu into a large bowl, making sure there are no chunks any larger than the size of peas. Add the basil, lemon juice, nutritional yeast, miso paste, olive oil, onion powder, garlic powder, and salt. Stir thoroughly to combine. This can be prepped well in advance and stored in the fridge in an airtight container for up to a week, if needed.

Spread 1 cup of the marinara sauce evenly across the bottom of your prepared sheet pan, making sure it reaches to the corners for full coverage, even if it's a thin coating. Top with a layer of lavash, cutting the pieces to fit if needed. Spread another cup of sauce on top, followed by half of the tofu ricotta. Cover with a second layer of lavash, the remaining sauce, and the last of the ricotta.

Bake for 25 to 30 minutes, until the top of the ricotta is lightly golden, and the lasagna is hot all the way through. Cut into generous rectangles and serve.

> **Feeling cheesy?** Ramp up the ooey-gooey cheese factor by sprinkling 1 to 2 cups of shredded vegan mozzarella on top right before baking.

LOW COUNTRY BROIL

MAKES 4 TO 6 SERVINGS

The original one-pot meal for the masses, southerners have long gathered around this giant steaming supper for get-togethers, family reunions, and summer holidays. The true origins can be traced back further to the Gullah people along the coasts of Georgia and South Carolina. Africans in the slave trade had brought with them not only cooking influences from their homeland, but Spanish and French cooking influences as well. Meals for large groups of people could be made as quickly as possible with readily available foods; mostly seafood and starchy vegetables at the time. Designed to be quick and easy, the real "work" begins when it's time to eat! Roll up your sleeves and dig right in; this is no place for forks or knives. If you're not wearing at least part of your meal by the end, you're not doing it right.

Employing more plants and much less water, my sheet pan version is made with the same free-spirited enthusiasm. Seared from the top down under blisteringly high heat, I'm broiling this cornucopia of summer produce, not boiling. Rather than washing away those vital nutrients and flavors, they remain intact, and more vibrant than ever.

2 tablespoons olive oil

1 red onion, halved and sliced

1 pound red-skinned baby potatoes, quartered

4 ears corn, husked and quartered

8 ounces meatless sausage, seitan, or tempeh, sliced into ½-inch pieces

1 (14-ounce) can sliced hearts of palm, drained

1 pound green beans, trimmed

1 cup vegetable stock

2 tablespoons Old Bay seasoning

1 tablespoon whole mustard seeds

1 tablespoon whole coriander seeds

2 teaspoons smoked paprika

1 teaspoon whole allspice berries

¼ teaspoon cayenne pepper

2 bay leaves

½ cup vegan butter, to serve

Adjust an oven rack into the top position and preheat the broiler to high.

Rub a half sheet pan with 1 tablespoon of oil, coating the bottom thoroughly. Scatter the onion, potatoes, corn, and meatless protein on top, distributing the pieces equally and evenly. Place it under the broiler and let cook for 10 minutes.

Flip all the vegetables and proteins and run them back under the broiler for another 5 minutes.

Pull out the sheet again to add the hearts of palm and green beans, pushing the other pieces closer to give the fresh additions full contact with the bottom of the hot sheet. Drizzle with the remaining oil and return the sheet to the oven. Broil for another 5 minutes.

Meanwhile, whisk together the vegetable stock, Old Bay seasoning, mustard seeds, coriander seeds, paprika, allspice berries, cayenne, and bay leaves in a medium dish. Carefully pour the seasoning liquid all over the vegetables and proteins, moving the sheet pan around as little as possible to prevent splashes or spills.

Finally, broil for 8 to 10 minutes longer, until the potatoes are fork tender and everything is golden-brown. Transfer to a serving platter or set the whole sheet pan right on the table. Serve with melted vegan butter alongside to dip as desired.

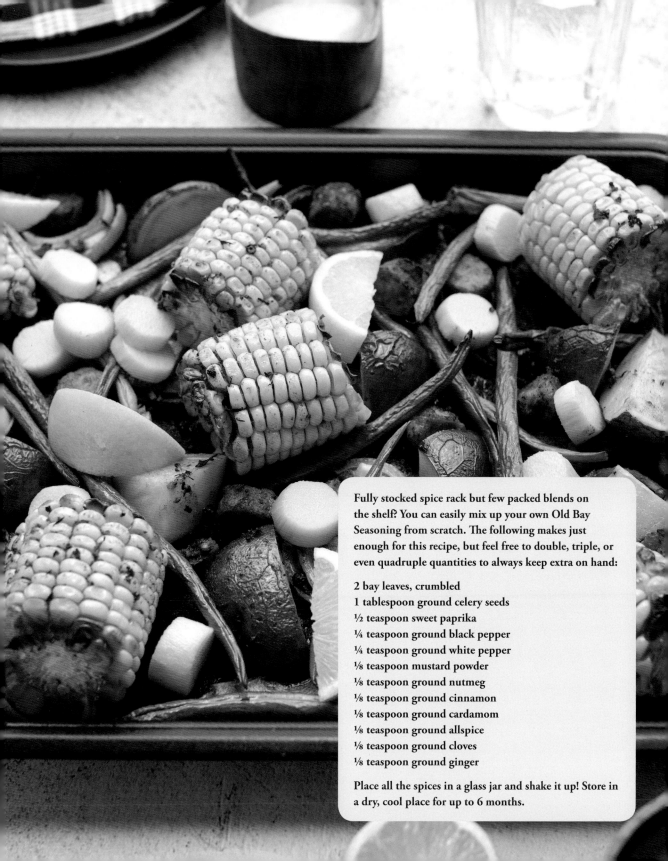

Fully stocked spice rack but few packed blends on the shelf? You can easily mix up your own Old Bay Seasoning from scratch. The following makes just enough for this recipe, but feel free to double, triple, or even quadruple quantities to always keep extra on hand:

2 bay leaves, crumbled
1 tablespoon ground celery seeds
½ teaspoon sweet paprika
¼ teaspoon ground black pepper
¼ teaspoon ground white pepper
⅛ teaspoon mustard powder
⅛ teaspoon ground nutmeg
⅛ teaspoon ground cinnamon
⅛ teaspoon ground cardamom
⅛ teaspoon ground allspice
⅛ teaspoon ground cloves
⅛ teaspoon ground ginger

Place all the spices in a glass jar and shake it up! Store in a dry, cool place for up to 6 months.

MAD MAC & PEAS

MAKES 6 TO 8 SERVINGS

You would have to be mad to make mac and cheese in the oven, without a pot, and without cooking the noodles first. Welcome to the looney bin! It turns out that this crazy quick fix turns out even better than your typical stovetop mac. Instead of draining away the rich starch from the noodles, it creates a thick, voluptuous sauce without making a roux. You get all the saucy goodness within plus impeccably crisp breadcrumbs across the whole sheet, so no one needs to fight over the illustrious corner pieces. It's said that madness and genius are closely related; perhaps that's why this recipe is just crazy enough to work!

½ cup vegan butter, melted and divided
½ cup pumpkin puree
⅓ cup nutritional yeast
¼ cup tapioca starch
1 tablespoon Dijon mustard
1 teaspoon onion powder
1 teaspoon smoked paprika
½ teaspoon garlic powder
½ teaspoon salt
¼ teaspoon ground turmeric
2½ cups unsweetened non-dairy milk
12 ounces dry elbow macaroni
1½ cups green peas, fresh or frozen and thawed
¾ cup breadcrumbs

Position an oven rack into the center and preheat to 375°F.

Prepare the cheese sauce by pouring the first 6 tablespoons of the melted vegan butter into a large bowl. Add the pumpkin puree, nutritional yeast, tapioca starch, mustard, onion powder, smoked paprika, garlic powder, salt, and turmeric. Stir vigorously to create a thick, smooth, orange paste. Make sure there are no clumps of dry ingredients remaining. Slowly whisk in the non-dairy milk, incorporating all the seasonings into a homogeneous blend about the consistency of pancake batter.

Lightly grease a non-stick half sheet pan. Scatter the dry pasta on top, spreading out the pieces in an even layer. Sprinkle the peas over next, distributing them as equally as possible across the surface. Pour the cheese sauce all over and cover with aluminum foil.

Very carefully move the sheet pan into the oven. Bake for 25 minutes.

Meanwhile, combine the breadcrumbs and remaining melted vegan butter in a medium bowl. Stir to coat and set aside.

Uncover the macaroni, removing the foil entirely, and sprinkle the breadcrumb mixture all over. Return the sheet to the oven and bake for another 15 to 20 minutes, until golden-brown on top and the noodles are tender. Let stand for at least 10 minutes before serving.

PAELLA HUERTA

MAKES 6 TO 8 SERVINGS

Huerta means orchard or vegetable garden, so it stands to reason that this paella is packed full of fresh vegetables and vibrant yellow grains of rice, all infused with saffron. Redolent of onions and garlic, it's a simple yet classic dish that must not be underestimated. The beauty of this dish is that it's endlessly versatile, and pretty much any vegetables hanging out in the fridge will do just fine. Consider throwing in a drained and rinsed can of chickpeas for a bit more protein, too.

3 tablespoons olive oil, divided
½ large red onion, diced
2 cups cremini or button mushrooms, halved
3 cloves garlic, minced
1 teaspoon salt, divided
1 medium red, orange, or yellow bell pepper, seeded and sliced into 1-inch lengths
1 medium zucchini, halved lengthwise and sliced ¼-inch thick
¼ pound green beans, trimmed and sliced into 1-inch lengths
1½ cups medium grain rice
4 cups vegetable stock
1 teaspoon smoked paprika
¼ teaspoon ground black pepper
⅛ teaspoon saffron threads, crushed
1 (14-ounce) can quartered artichoke hearts, drained
1 cups frozen peas
1 lemon, sliced into wedges

Preheat your oven to 375°F. Drizzle half of the olive oil on half sheet pan, tilting it around to coat the bottom.

Distribute the onions, mushrooms, and garlic on top of the pan before sprinkling with half of the salt. Roast for 15 minutes, stirring about halfway through the process. The onions should be aromatic, and the mushrooms considerably softened.

Add the pepper, zucchini, and green beans right on top. Bake for another 10 minutes, mix well, and sprinkle the rice over all the vegetables. Place the sheet on the upper rack of the oven to toast the rice; just 5 minutes or so until lightly golden around the edges.

Meanwhile, whisk together the vegetable stock, paprika, pepper, saffron, and the remaining oil and salt. Once the rice is toasted, carefully pour the liquid seasoning mixture all over, and stir well to incorporate, covering all the grains of rice. Cover with foil and return to the oven.

Lower the heat to 350°F and cook for 35 to 40 minutes longer, until the liquid has mostly been absorbed. Remove the foil, add the artichoke hearts and frozen peas, and cook for a final 5 minutes, just to thaw out and warm the peas. Stir well to incorporate before transferring everything to a serving platter.

Serve with lemon wedges on the side.

Dig deep into your vegetable garden, or produce bin, as it may be, to mix and match ingredients for a bold new harvest every time. A few of my favorite alternative additions are halved Brussels sprouts, fava beans, asparagus, olives, cauliflower, diced tomatoes, snow peas, and baby carrots, just to name a few. On the other hand, if mother nature doesn't have much to offer in the way of fresh selections, feel free to use any blend of frozen you've got chilling out. Just thaw before using and aim for a total of 4 to 6 cups of produce all told.

PORTOBELLO PAPRIKASH

MAKES 4 SERVINGS

When I went vegan, despite what my culinary background might suggest, I was not the least bit interested in food. In fact, I was a terribly picky eater, shunning all green vegetables, most fruits, and yes, any sort of meat that resembled the original animal. It wasn't hard to make the switch because I barely ate anything to begin with!

Prior to that moment, however, one dish that would bring everyone to the table was chicken paprika. Despite the difficulties posed by two fussy children and one equally discerning husband, my mom did enjoy cooking, and tried repeatedly to find something that we could all eat together, in health and happiness.

It's incredibly basic, as the most comforting dishes tend to be. In tough times, when I miss my parents, my cozy home back on the east coast, and all the tenderness they showed me as I grew into a self-sufficient little herbivore, I do crave these flavors. Swapping out the meat is effortless now, thanks to the rapidly expanding array of plant-based options in stores.

I still don't miss the chicken one bit. All I'm missing now is the company.

PAPRIKASH:
- ¼ pound (½ package) soy curls
- 2 cups boiling water
- 3 tablespoons olive oil, divided
- 1 medium yellow onion, diced
- ½ pound (about 2 medium) portobello caps, stems removed
- ½ teaspoon salt
- 1 cup vegetable stock
- 1 tablespoon tomato paste
- 1 tablespoon sweet paprika
- 1 teaspoon hot paprika
- 1 teaspoon smoked paprika
- 2 teaspoons cornstarch

TO SERVE:
- 2–4 cups cooked pasta, rice, or potatoes (optional)

Preheat your oven to 375°F.

Place the soy curls in a medium bowl and pour the boiling water on top. Let sit and soak for about 15 to 20 minutes until rehydrated. Drain away any excess water.

Meanwhile, coat a half sheet pan with 1 tablespoon of the oil. Add the onion on top and slide the sheet into the oven to bake for 5 to 6 minutes, until softened and translucent.

Arrange the sliced mushrooms on top. Drizzle with another tablespoon of the oil and sprinkle evenly with salt. Bake for 6 to 8 minutes, until they begin to wilt.

Add the soy curls on top of the heap along with the final tablespoon of oil. Cook for 15 to 20 minutes, until lightly browned around the edges.

Meanwhile, in a separate dish, whisk together the vegetable stock, tomato paste, all three types of paprika, and cornstarch. Pour this liquid seasoning mixture all over the vegetables and protein, stirring to thoroughly coat. Roast for a final 10 to 15 minutes, stirring halfway through, until the liquid has been absorbed and everything is a deep ruby red.

Serve immediately over cooked pasta, rice, or potatoes, if desired.

SHEET LOAF WITH MASHED CAULIFLOWER

MAKES 8 SERVINGS

What could be more American than meatloaf? Apple pie can't hold a candle to such quintessential home cooking, a tried-and-true staple throughout the ages. Though it really took off in the Great Depression as a thrifty way of stretching meager portions of protein, the earliest example traces back to the fourth or fifth century in ancient Rome, making it yet another import we owe to brilliant immigrants from across the globe.

Truth be told, meatloaf appreciation must be a recessive gene, because I can't even recall eating it once as a kid. To compensate for my squandered youth, I'm making up for lost time with a kinder, gentler, and quite frankly, tastier, legume loaf instead. Maximizing the umami of tomatoes and herbs paired with a subtle sweetness, this recipe revamp yields more tender, moist, plant-powered slices.

One cannot live on loaf alone, which is why mashed cauliflower is a perfect lower-carb sidekick to lighten the load. Whether chopped coarsely or pureed to a smooth, silky submission, it makes a complete meal on one sheet. Meet—or should I say "meat"—your new nostalgic family favorite.

ROASTED MASHED CAULIFLOWER:

1 large head cauliflower (about 1¾–2 pounds), cut into florets (stem included)

¼ cup olive oil, divided

½ teaspoon salt

¼ teaspoon ground black pepper

⅓–½ cup plain, unsweetened non-dairy milk

MEATLESS LOAF:

2 (15-ounce) cans (3 cups cooked) red kidney beans, drained and rinsed

4 cloves garlic, minced

½ cup sundried tomatoes, roughly chopped

1 (8-ounce) can (1 cup) tomato sauce, divided

1 tablespoon soy sauce

1 teaspoon apple cider vinegar

½ teaspoon liquid smoke

2 tablespoons ground flaxseeds

1 tablespoon coconut sugar or dark brown sugar, firmly packed

1 tablespoon dried parsley

1 teaspoon dry mustard powder

1 teaspoon dried thyme

½ teaspoon dried rosemary

¼ teaspoon dried sage, crumbled

½ teaspoon salt

½ teaspoon ground black pepper

1¼ cups panko breadcrumbs

Preheat your oven to 400°F and lightly grease a half sheet pan.

Begin by prepping the cauliflower. Toss the florets and pieces with 2 tablespoons of olive oil, salt, and pepper and spread them out in an even layer on just half of the sheet pan. If it's too much to fit neatly in only part of the available space, use a separate quarter sheet pan for the loaf.

(Continued on page 182)

For the loaf, place the beans in a large bowl and roughly mash them with a potato masher. The mixture should be coarse and chunky, not totally smooth. It should have a decent amount of texture left so that the loaf has a satisfying bite when served. Add in the garlic, sundried tomatoes, ¾ cups of the tomato sauce, soy sauce, vinegar, liquid smoke, flaxseeds, sugar, parsley, mustard powder, thyme, rosemary, sage, salt, and pepper. Stir well to combine.

Add in the panko last, folding gently with a wide spatula to incorporate. The mixture should be thick enough to shape into a loaf, which is exactly what you need to do next!

Transfer the mixture to the empty half of your prepared sheet pan, smoothing it into a roughly 8 × 4-inch rectangle. Make sure it's not touching any of the cauliflower.

Bake in the center of your oven for 30 minutes. Carefully remove the pan and brush the top of the loaf with the remaining ¼ cup of tomato sauce. Return it to the oven and bake for a final 12 to 15 minutes, until the cauliflower is golden-brown, and the loaf is set.

Transfer the cauliflower to a large bowl along with ⅓ cup of non-dairy milk and the remaining 2 tablespoons of oil. Mash vigorously with a potato masher or pastry cutter for a coarse texture, or transfer to a food processor and pulse until smooth. Add more non-dairy milk as needed to reach your desired consistency.

Let the loaf rest for 10 to 15 minutes before slicing. Serve alongside the mashed cauliflower and enjoy hot.

Tired of the typical loaf? Spice things up with a picadillo-inspired variation. Add ½ cup finely diced green bell pepper, ⅓ cup sliced green olives, ¼ cup raisins, 1 teaspoon ground cumin, and ½ teaspoon dried oregano to the meatless mixture.

SHEET PAN PIZZA

MAKES 16 SERVINGS

As a kid, thin crust was the only kind of pizza in my life. Everything else was just glorified round bread with sauce on top. Further spoiled by a native New Yorker as a father, we would roll out our own crust at home on special occasions, stretching the very limits of gluten itself into sheets practically translucent enough to read a newspaper through. Though this is still the gold standard of pizza in my opinion, I've found room in my heart, and stomach, for crusts of all kinds.

Thick, buttery, chewy, and blistered across the bottom, pan pizza can also be considered deep-dish pizza depending on where you grew up. Arguably easier to perfect, it isn't as demanding or laborious to finesse into shape; it's even simpler than making a loaf of bread. It's the solid, supportive base we all need sometimes to accommodate all the toppings of our dreams. Go wild, pile it on thick, and don't let anyone tell you what can and can't be a proper pizza.

PIZZA DOUGH:
1¼ cups warm water
1 (¼-ounce) packet (1¾ teaspoons)
    active dry yeast
1 teaspoon granulated sugar
¾ teaspoon salt
3½–4 cups all-purpose flour
2 tablespoons + ¼ cup olive oil,
    divided

ALMOND PARMESAN:
¾ cup blanched almond flour
¼ cup nutritional yeast
½ teaspoon salt
¼ teaspoon garlic powder

TO ASSEMBLE:
1 cup tomato sauce or pizza sauce
1 cup fresh spinach
¼ cup sliced black olives
¼ cup thinly sliced red onions
½ cup sliced mushrooms

In the bowl of your stand mixer, combine the water, yeast, and sugar. Let stand for 10 to 15 minutes, until the yeast reactivates and becomes slightly frothy.

Add the salt, 3 cups of the flour, and 2 tablespoons of the oil. Install the dough hook and begin mixing on low speed until combined. Pause to scrape down the bowl with your spatula as needed, to make sure everything is smoothly incorporated.

Add the remaining flour, ½ cup at a time, until dough comes together and forms a soft, smooth ball. Continue to knead with the dough hook for about 10 minutes. The dough should be elastic but not wet or sticky.

Transfer to a lightly greased bowl and cover with a clean kitchen towel. Let rest in a warm, draft-free place for about an hour, or until roughly doubled in size.

Preheat your oven to 475°F.

You can make either one large sheet pan pizza or two smaller pizzas, which is handy for serving a crowd with diverse tastes. Drizzle the remaining ¼ cup of oil all over a half sheet pan or two quarter sheet pans, depending on which route you'd like to take. Make sure the bottom and sides are thoroughly coated.

(Continued on page 185)

Transfer the dough into the oiled pan(s) and use lightly moistened hands to press it evenly across the bottom, gently stretching, kneading, and poking it to fill the entire space. If it starts to fight back, let it rest for a few minutes before stretching it again.

Let rest for 20 to 30 minutes to rise once more. Use your knuckles to dimple the dough across the surface, redistributing any air bubbles evenly throughout.

Bake for 10 minutes, until lightly browned—you don't want to fully bake the crust at this stage. Spread the tomato sauce on top, leaving a narrow margin around the border clean. Sprinkle the spinach, olives, onion, and mushrooms at random, distributing them as evenly as possible.

Meanwhile, prepare the almond Parmesan by simply combining the almond flour, nutritional yeast, salt, and garlic powder in a small dish.

Return the pizza(s) to the oven for a final 8 to 12 minutes, until the crust is crisp, slightly blistered, and darkly browned underneath. Sprinkle generously with the almond Parmesan, slice, and serve hot!

The world of pizza toppings is vast as the universe itself. If you can dream it, it can become a pizza, too! Trust me, I've even seen tapioca pearls as a real option on savory pies overseas. For more crowd-pleasing combinations, I might suggest . . .

> Vegan cheese shreds or sauce
> Diced pineapple
> Roasted garlic
> Fresh tomatoes, sliced
> Roasted eggplant
> Pine nuts
> Coconut bacon
> Artichoke hearts
> Fresh basil
> Arugula

. . . Just for starters!

SOY CURL BULGOGI WITH BROCCOLI

MAKES 4 SERVINGS

Sizzling and sputtering violently beneath high heat, the best bulgogi is an all-out assault on the senses. It speaks loudly, radiating with pungent spices, taking on an eerily life-like quality as steam envelops the dish. Breathing in fiery aroma from a mile away, you'll know it's coming long before it hits the table. This arresting experience is typically the result of hours of marinating, but by rehydrating soy curls right in the brine, you'll effortlessly infuse those flavors right into the very core of the "meat." The crispy bits around the edges are the best parts, which will be in no shortage thanks to the expansive sheet of hot metal supporting this blazingly fast meal.

4 ounces (½ package) dry soy curls
3 cups warm water
1 tablespoon pomegranate molasses
1 medium head broccoli, cut into
    florets
1 medium onion, sliced
¼ cup soy sauce
1 tablespoon rice vinegar
1 tablespoon toasted sesame oil
1 tablespoon olive oil
1 tablespoon coconut sugar or light
    brown sugar, firmly packed
1 tablespoon minced fresh ginger
2 cloves garlic, finely minced
2 teaspoons gochugaru (Korean hot
    pepper flakes) or 1–1½ teaspoons
    crushed red pepper flakes
1 teaspoon sesame seeds
1 scallion, thinly sliced

Place the dry soy curls in a large bowl and cover with warm water. Mix in the pomegranate molasses and let sit for 20 to 30 minutes, until fully rehydrated.

Meanwhile, preheat your oven to 375°F.

Drain away the excess liquid. Return the softened soy curls to the bowl, along with the broccoli and onion. Add in the soy sauce, vinegar, sesame and olive oil, sugar, ginger, garlic, and hot pepper flakes. Toss thoroughly to coat everything with the marinade. Allow at least 10 minutes for the flavorful liquid to soak in.

Transfer the contents of the bowl to an ungreased sheet pan, spreading the protein and vegetables out into one even layer, overlapping as little as possible. Bake for about 30 minutes, until the broccoli is lightly charred, and the onions are tender. Sprinkle with sesame seeds and sliced scallion just prior to serving.

Enjoy solo, over rice, noodles, or in lettuce wraps.

SPAGHETTI SQUASH BOLOGNESE

MAKES 4 SERVINGS

While pasta always has a place in my heart (and pantry), it's fun to switch up the usual routine with some truly plant-based noodles. Spaghetti squash has the added benefit of tenderizing in the oven, cooking right alongside the thick and hearty meatless ragu. Deeply comforting, endlessly versatile, the Bolognese sauce will serve you well no matter what sort of red sauce you're craving. Omit the nuts and lentils for a simple marinara or add a splash of coconut milk for a creamier concoction.

1 medium (2¾–3 pounds) spaghetti squash

2 tablespoons olive oil, divided

¾ teaspoon salt, divided

1 medium (8 ounces) red beet, peeled and finely diced (about 1 cup)

4 cloves garlic, minced

½ cup raw walnuts, roughly chopped

2 cups marinara sauce

1 (14-ounce) can (1½ cups cooked) brown lentils, drained

2 tablespoons tomato paste

2 tablespoons nutritional yeast

⅓ cup fresh basil, minced

¼ cup fresh parsley, minced

¼ teaspoon crushed red pepper flakes

Don't squander those seeds! Rather than tossing them into the compost, you can turn them into a tasty snack. Clean off any excess membrane from the squash and toss them with a touch of olive oil, salt, and pepper. Roast at 300°F for 30 to 40 minutes, stirring every 15 minutes or so, until golden and crisp. Let cool and snack happy!

Preheat your oven to 400°F.

Cut the spaghetti squash in half lengthwise and use a sturdy spoon to scoop out the seeds and membrane. Coat the halves with ½ tablespoon of olive oil each, rubbing it all over the interior. Sprinkle evenly with ¼ teaspoon of salt and place them cut sides down on a half sheet pan.

Roast for 30 to 40 minutes, until lightly browned on the outside, fork tender, but still slightly firm. The time will vary depending on the size of your squash. Remove from the sheet pan and set aside until cool enough to handle; about 10 minutes.

Meanwhile, coat the sheet pan with the remaining tablespoon of olive oil. Toss together the diced beet and garlic on top, along with ¼ teaspoon of salt. Return the pan to the oven and bake for 10 to 15 minutes, until the beets are tender, and the garlic is highly aromatic. Add the walnuts and toast for just 5 minutes.

Pour the marinara sauce all over, followed by the lentils. Stir the tomato paste in and nutritional yeast, and toss to thoroughly incorporate and distribute all the components. Bake for a final 5 to 8 minutes, until hot all the way through. Mix in the remaining ¼ teaspoon of salt, basil, parsley, and red pepper last.

To serve, scrape the interior of the spaghetti squash with a fork to pull out the tender strands. Either place in a large serving bowl and top with the hot Bolognese sauce, or pile it all on top of the sauce and serve straight from the sheet pan.

SWEET SESAME TOFU AND ROASTED BRUSSELS SPROUTS

MAKES 4 TO 6 SERVINGS

Lay out all your vegetables and tofu at once and just let it roast for an effortless, deeply satisfying complete dinner. After some quick prep, you'll end up with beautifully burnished, fork-tender Brussels sprouts, crispy cubes of tofu, and a sticky, savory glaze to coat it all. How's that for a hands-off meal?

TOFU AND BRUSSELS SPROUTS:

1 (14-ounce) package extra-firm tofu, drained and cut into ½-inch cubes
2 tablespoons arrowroot powder
1½ tablespoons toasted sesame oil, divided
3 tablespoons low-sodium soy sauce
3 tablespoons maple syrup
1 tablespoon balsamic vinegar
1 clove garlic, finely minced
1 pound Brussels sprouts, trimmed and halved
¼ teaspoon ground black pepper

TO SERVE:

2–3 cups cooked brown rice
2 tablespoons toasted sesame seeds

Preheat your oven to 400°F and grab a nonstick baking sheet; set aside.

Lightly blot the tofu with a paper towel or clean dish towel to absorb as much excess water as possible before tossing the cubes together with the arrowroot. Coat as evenly as possible, shaking off any extra. Spread the pieces out on half of the baking sheet in one even layer and drizzle with ½ tablespoon sesame oil.

In a large bowl, whisk together the soy sauce, maple syrup, balsamic vinegar, garlic, and remaining tablespoon of sesame oil. Add in the sprouts and stir thoroughly. Transfer to the empty side of your baking sheet, along with all the leftover marinade. Don't worry that it seems like a lot of liquid, or that it will likely run over and touch the tofu; it will reduce in the oven and become a rich, delicious sauce to cover everything. Sprinkle the whole sheet lightly with black pepper.

Bake for 25 minutes, until the sprouts are fork tender and lightly browned. Turn on the broiler to high and cook for an additional 5 minutes to perfectly crisp up the edges of the tofu.

To serve, stir the vegetables and protein together to combine and coat with the thick glaze at the bottom of the baking sheet. Sprinkle with sesame seeds and serve alongside hot steamed rice.

TEMPEH PICCATA

MAKES 2 TO 3 SERVINGS

Lavished with a lemon-caper sauce that could make any protein shine, this tempeh will make you pucker up, and not just because of that lush, briny marinade! Everyone will fall in love at first bite, especially considering how quickly and easily this full meal comes together. Paired with baby potatoes and asparagus cooked right alongside, it's a perfect date meal, family dinner, or everyday sort of indulgence. Little salty explosions punctuate the garlicky landscape thanks to those pickled flower buds, which are essential to the dish. Some say green olives will work in a pinch, but I'd implore you to seek out the real deal. Capers are readily available in all grocery stores and last forever in the pantry—in theory, at least. This recipe is one I tend to eat on repeat, so you might want to buy the bigger bottle, just in case.

¼ cup olive oil
1 (8-ounce) package tempeh
1 medium shallot or ½ medium yellow onion, thinly sliced
2 cloves garlic, thinly sliced
¾ pound red baby potatoes
¼ cup white wine
¼ cup lemon juice
¼ cup low-sodium vegetable stock
1 tablespoon tapioca starch
2 teaspoons nutritional yeast
¼ teaspoon ground black pepper
¾ pound asparagus or green beans, trimmed
2 tablespoons capers, thoroughly drained
¼ cup fresh parsley, minced

> If you're not feeling tempted by tempeh, you can use extra-firm tofu or your favorite meatless chicken cutlets instead.

Preheat your oven to 400°F and coat a half sheet pan generously with the oil.

Cut the tempeh into 3 equal rectangles, and then slice each of those rectangles in half diagonally to end up with 6 triangles. Arrange the pieces neatly on one end of the sheet pan. Spread the shallot or onion in a line alongside, topped by the sliced garlic.

Slice the potatoes in half and cut halves into quarters. Spread the chunks out in the center of pan, next to the line of alliums, without overlapping.

Bake for 15 minutes, until the protein is beginning to brown around the edges. Flip the tempeh, stir the potatoes, and add the white wine. Return the pan to the oven for another 5 minutes.

Meanwhile, combine the lemon juice, vegetable stock, tapioca starch, nutritional yeast, and black pepper in a small dish.

Carefully pour the liquid seasoning mixture all over and add the asparagus on the remaining empty space at the end of the sheet pan. Cook for 10 to 15 minutes longer, until the vegetables are fork-tender, and everything is golden-brown.

Mix the aromatics together with the tempeh, adding in the capers and parsley just before serving. Distribute equal portions onto plates and dig in.

TOFU FRIED RICE

Rock out without your wok out! Fried rice comes together in a flash with a sheet pan. The key to transcendent fried rice is having a large playing field to prevent crowding the ingredients, since you need full surface contact to get the ideal sear. That's why the accommodating plane of a half sheet pan is even better suited to the task than a mere skillet or sauté pan. The order of operations is critical to make sure that everything is thoroughly cooked, satisfyingly charred, and not burnt. Start with the protein and hard root vegetables since they take the longest to cook. Make sure everything is prepped and close at hand to fry up a blazing hot meal even faster than your local Chinese restaurant can deliver.

- 3 tablespoons olive oil, divided
- 2 medium carrots, peeled and diced
- 1 (14-ounce) package extra-firm tofu, thoroughly drained and cut into ¼-inch cubes
- 4 cups cooked long grain brown or white rice, chilled
- ¼ cup soy sauce
- 3 cloves garlic, minced
- 1 inch fresh ginger, peeled and finely minced
- 2 teaspoons toasted sesame oil
- ½ teaspoon ground white pepper
- ½ cup frozen green peas
- 3 scallions, thinly sliced

Preheat your oven to 375°F and rub down a half sheet pan with 1 tablespoon of the olive oil. Scatter the diced carrots and tofu on top, spreading them out into an even layer. Bake for 18 to 20 minutes in the center of the oven, stirring halfway through, until lightly caramelized around the edges.

Pull the sheet pan out and add the rice, remaining olive oil, soy sauce, garlic, ginger, sesame oil, and white pepper. Stir well, taking care to incorporate the carrots and tofu while thoroughly distributing the seasonings throughout. Return the sheet to the oven on the top rack, and bake for an additional 15 to 18 minutes, without stirring. This will allow the rice to get nice and crispy on the bottom, rather than merely warmed through.

Add the peas right on top, no need to thaw, and bake for just a minute longer. Stir thoroughly to combine, top with scallions, and serve hot.

The variations for fried rice are endless! It would be easy to make a different version every day of the week without getting bored. This is just the basic blueprint, waiting for your creative embellishments. Here are a few of my favorites:

Korean Fried Rice: Roughly chop 2 cups fresh kimchi and add it within the final 5 minutes of cooking to spice things up.

Thai Fried Rice: For those who like a little sweet and savory twist, mix in 1 cup diced pineapple or mango right after the rice comes out of the oven, along with ¼ cup finely minced fresh basil.

Multigrain Fried Rice: Swap out any amount, or even all, of the rice for a blend of cooked quinoa, wheat berries, millet, and/or pearl barley.

Cauliflower Fried "Rice": Go grainless! Replace the rice with riced cauliflower. Just reduce the baking time to about 8 to 10 minutes once it goes into the oven.

DESSERT

APRICOT-ALMOND CLAFOUTIS

MAKES 8 TO 10 SERVINGS

Part custard, part pancake, the classic French clafoutis is an enigma of a dessert. Soft enough to serve with a spoon, but substantial enough to warrant a fork, it defines easy definition. Even the name could throw the casual eater, for such a fancy-sounding title. In truth, it's a rather humble sort of dish, effortless to whip up, featuring fresh fruit at the peak of perfection.

1¼ cups plain non-dairy milk
1 cup plain, unsweetened vegan
    yogurt
¾ cup granulated sugar
3 tablespoons vegan butter or
    coconut oil, melted
1 teaspoon orange zest
1 teaspoon vanilla extract
½ teaspoon almond extract
1 cup all-purpose flour
½ cup coarse almond meal
½ teaspoon salt
¼ teaspoon baking powder
5 medium (about 1 pound) apricots,
    pitted and sliced
¼ cup sliced almonds
Confectioners' sugar, to serve
    (optional)

Preheat your oven to 350°F and lightly grease a half sheet pan.

In a large bowl, whisk together the non-dairy milk, yogurt, sugar, melted butter or oil, zest, and both extracts. Stir until smooth and homogenous.

Separately, sift the flour, almond meal, salt, and baking powder. Pour the liquid ingredients into the bowl of dry, and stir just enough to bring the batter together, being careful not to over-mix; a few errant lumps are perfectly fine. The resulting texture should be very thin, much like pancake or crepe batter.

Transfer the batter to your prepared pan, smoothing it out into an even layer. Scatter the sliced apricots and almonds evenly across the top.

Bake for 26 to 28 minutes until lightly golden-brown around the edges. Let rest for at least 15 minutes or until cool enough to handle; don't worry if it seems to deflate during that time. Slice into square or rectangles, dust with confectioners' sugar if desired, and enjoy warm or at room temperature.

> **Apricots nowhere to be found? Don't fret; you can vary the fruit to suit anything currently in season. Peaches, plums, and cherries in particular are all exceptional choices.**

BROWNIE CRISPS

MAKES 2 TO 2½ DOZEN BROWNIE CRISPS

For anyone who's fought to get the corner piece from a pan of fudgy brownies or relished the distinctive crackled top, these crisps have your name written all over them. Deceptively light, it's disturbingly easy to munch straight through half a batch without even pausing to take a breath.

⅓ cup aquafaba

½ cup granulated sugar

½ cup all-purpose flour

2 tablespoons Dutch-process cocoa powder

1 tablespoon unflavored pea or soy protein

¼ teaspoon instant coffee granules

¼ teaspoon salt

¼ teaspoon baking powder

¼ cup olive oil

½ cup (3 ounces) semi-sweet chocolate chips, divided

3 tablespoons chopped walnuts, divided

Blondies may or may not have more fun, but they're a delightful change of pace, regardless! Turn these crunchy cookies into blondie crisps by replacing the cocoa with an equal measure of protein powder and use brown sugar instead of granulated. For a complete blonde makeover, trade the dark chocolate chips for vegan white chocolate chips, too.

Preheat your oven to 300°F and line a half sheet pan with a piece of parchment paper or a silicone baking mat.

In a large bowl, combine the aquafaba and sugar and beat vigorously with a whisk until foamy. You're not looking to whip it into a firm meringue here, but a loose froth with the sugar fully dissolved. In a separate bowl, whisk together the flour, cocoa, protein, instant coffee, salt, and baking powder, stirring to ensure that all the ingredients are equally distributed throughout the mixture.

Slowly add in the dry ingredients while mixing, scraping down the sides of the bowl as needed. Immediately follow with the oil and stir just until the batter comes together smoothly. Fold in half of the chocolate chips and walnuts gently.

Transfer the batter to your prepared sheet pan and use an offset spatula to spread it out as thinly as possible. The batter should just about cover the whole sheet. Sprinkle the remaining chocolate chips and walnuts evenly over the top.

Bake on the center rack in the oven for 20 minutes, rotate the pan, and continue baking for 10 more minutes. Pull the sheet out and use a pizza cutter to slice the square or rectangular shapes you desire, but don't separate them yet. Return the cookies to the oven and bake for a final 10 to 14 minutes. They may still feel slightly soft in the center, but they'll continue to crisp as they cool.

Let the crisps cool completely on the baking sheet before breaking the cookies apart. Store in an airtight container for up to a week, if you can manage to keep them around that long.

CARROT CAKE ROULADE

MAKES 12 TO 16 SERVINGS

Gently spiced and speckled with orange flecks of carrot, this new take on carrot cake will send you spinning! Instead of smearing rich cream cheese frosting on the outside, that essential schmear is wrapped up in a spiral around the center. One might even feel slightly virtuous selecting a slice or two for breakfast, since you're getting a nice serving of vegetables, right?

CARROT CAKE:

¼ cup aquafaba
¼ cup granulated sugar
½ cup carrot puree
¾ cup plain non-dairy milk
2 tablespoons olive oil
¼ cup dark brown sugar, firmly packed
1 cup finely shredded carrot (about 1 medium carrot)
1 teaspoon vanilla extract
1 teaspoon apple cider vinegar
1 cup all-purpose flour, plus additional for dusting
1½ teaspoons ground cinnamon
1 teaspoon ground ginger
1 teaspoon baking powder
1 teaspoon baking soda
¼ teaspoon xanthan gum
¼ teaspoon salt

CREAM CHEESE FROSTING:

1 (8-ounce) package vegan cream cheese
5 tablespoons vegan butter
2 cups confectioners' sugar
2 teaspoons vanilla extract

TO ASSEMBLE:

½ cup chopped pecans or walnuts
¼ cup confectioners' sugar (optional)

Beginning with the cake, preheat your oven to 375°F and line a 10 × 15-inch jelly roll pan with parchment paper, making sure the edges are completely covered. It's important to use a baking sheet that's close to these dimensions or the cake will be too thick or thin to roll properly.

Pour the aquafaba into the bowl of your stand mixer with the whisk attachment installed and gradually increase the speed up to its highest setting. Once you have a steady froth going, slowly sprinkle in the granulated sugar, and then whip at full power for 5 to 7 minutes, until you achieve a sturdy meringue that stands up in firm peaks.

In a separate bowl, whisk together the carrot puree, non-dairy milk, oil, brown sugar, shredded carrots, vanilla, and vinegar. Stir until homogenous and emulsified.

Separately, sift together the flour, cinnamon, ginger, baking powder, baking soda, xanthan gum, and salt, blending until the dry ingredients are thoroughly distributed. Add this blend into the carrot mixture, stirring lightly until just combined.

Add about half of the whipped aquafaba, using a wide spatula to gently fold it in. Try to keep it light and airy, mixing just enough to combine without beating out all the air bubbles. Repeat the procedure with the remaining fluff.

Spread the batter out evenly across your prepared jelly roll pan. It may seem like a very thin layer but fear not! It shouldn't be very tall, as that would make it impossible to roll. Smooth out the top before sliding it into the oven.

(Continued on next page)

Bake for 15 to 18 minutes, or until firm but springy to the touch. Let cool for 5 minutes in the pan.

Use the edges of the parchment paper as a sling to gently lift the cake out of the pan. Lightly dust the top with additional flour and place a clean dish towel on top. Roll the cake lengthwise, from short end to short end, peeling away the parchment paper up and wrapping in the dish towel as you go. The cake will be the most fragile at this stage so try to keep it fairly loose and handle the cake as little as possible. Cool to room temperature before transferring to the fridge to chill.

While the cake cools, go ahead and prepare the cream cheese frosting. Simply beat together the cream cheese and vegan butter in the bowl of your stand mixer until smooth. Add in the confectioners' sugar and vanilla, and then whip on high speed for 3 to 5 minutes, until homogenous, light, and fluffy. Scrape down the sides of the bowl periodically to make sure that everything is fully incorporated.

To assemble, carefully unroll the cake and have it ready on the counter. Dollop spoonfuls of the frosting all over the cake, leaving about a ½-inch border along the edge. Smooth it into as even a layer as possible and sprinkle the chopped nuts all over.

Quickly but methodically begin rolling the cake back up the same way it was unrolled, from short end to short end. Some of the frosting may squish out of the ends, but just keep rolling!

Wrap the towel tightly around the filled roulade, twisting the ends and placing them underneath the cake. Place on a large plate or baking sheet and stash the whole thing on a flat surface in your fridge. Let set for at least an hour before serving.

For the final presentation, remove the towel and transfer to a serving platter, placing the seam-side down. Slice off the messy ends and lightly dust with confectioners' sugar, if desired. Stash back in the fridge until ready to slice and serve.

Think carrot puree will be hard to come by? Think again, and for that matter, look again! Check the baby food aisle for 100% carrot puree and you should be happily surprised. In a pinch, though, you can substitute canned pumpkin puree instead.

CHERRY-COLA TEXAS SHEET CAKE

MAKES 16 TO 20 SERVINGS

Coke is a catch-all term for soft drinks in the south, so it only makes sense to make actual cola the star of this Texan treat. Bubbling up in this potluck favorite, thin squares of cake the size of the Lone Star State are slathered in fudge-like icing. Once you sink your fork into it, the surface will crackle and give way to the soft, gooey chocolate underneath. Candied maraschino cherries punctuate the cake underneath, brightening the flavor profile far more than mere extracts ever could. The combination transcends all regional boundaries to create an effervescent delight everyone will love.

CHERRY-COLA SHEET CAKE:

1¼ cups light brown sugar, firmly packed

1 cup sugar-sweetened cola

⅔ cup olive oil

1 cup unsweetened applesauce

1 teaspoon apple cider vinegar

1 teaspoon vanilla extract

2 cups all-purpose flour

¼ cup Dutch-process cocoa powder

1 teaspoon baking powder

1 teaspoon baking soda

½ teaspoon salt

1 cup maraschino cherries, roughly chopped

COCOA-COLA FROSTING:

½ cup vegan butter, melted

3 cups confectioners' sugar

¼ cup Dutch-process cocoa powder

6 tablespoons sugar-sweetened cola

TO GARNISH (OPTIONAL):

¼ cup sprinkles or chopped nuts

Preheat your oven to 350°F and lightly grease a half sheet pan.

In a medium bowl, combine the sugar, cola, oil, applesauce, vinegar, and vanilla. Give the soda enough time to finish fizzing before adding it in, to make sure you get an accurate measurement. Set aside.

In a separate bowl, whisk together the flour, cocoa, baking powder and soda, and salt. Make sure all the ingredients are fully incorporated and no clumps of cocoa remain. Add the chopped cherries and toss to coat. This will help prevent them from simply sinking to the bottom of the cake while it bakes.

Pour the liquid ingredients into the bowlful of dry and stir with a wide spatula to incorporate. Mix just enough to bring the batter together; a few lumps are fine.

Transfer to your prepared sheet pan, smoothing the batter out to reach all the sides and corners evenly.

Bake for 14 to 18 minutes, until set. Check by inserting a toothpick into the center; it should pull out cleanly, with perhaps a few moist crumbs clinging to it, but not raw batter.

While the cake is in the oven, go ahead and prepare the icing. Place the melted vegan butter in a medium bowl and add in the confectioners' sugar and cocoa. Whisk vigorously to incorporate, beating out any possible clumps. Slowly add the cola while continuing to whisk, blending it into a smooth, thick, but easily pourable topping.

(Continued on page 207)

Pour the icing all over cake while it's still hot, fresh out of the oven. Use a spatula to spread it evenly over the cake, and finish with sprinkles or nuts, if desired. Let cool completely for the frosting to set before slicing and serving; at least 15 to 20 minutes.

The cake can be prepared in advance if covered and stored in an airtight container for 2 to 3 days at room temperature.

DOUBLE DARK FUDGEWICHES

MAKES 24 COOKIES; 12 SANDWICHES

Calling all chocoholics: Meet your new dark, decadent obsession. Thick, chewy, chocolatey cookie bars meet creamy no-churn ice cream in a single big batch. That means as tempting as it will be to hoard such treats, there's plenty to go around. The longer you can let the cookies sit with the frozen filling, the softer they'll get, creating a perfectly matched fudgy bite all the way through.

CHOCOLATE-CHOCOLATE CHIP COOKIE BARS:

¾ cup vegan butter or refined coconut oil, melted
1 cup dark brown sugar, firmly packed
½ cup granulated sugar
½ cup unsweetened applesauce
2 teaspoons vanilla extract
2½ cups all-purpose flour
½ cup Dutch-process cocoa powder
1 teaspoon salt
½ teaspoon baking powder
1 teaspoon baking soda
1 cup semi-sweet chocolate chips

NO CHURN CHOCOLATE ICE CREAM:

2 (14-ounce) cans full-fat coconut milk, chilled
⅔ cup confectioners' sugar
⅓ cup Dutch-process cocoa powder
½ teaspoon vanilla extract

Preheat your oven to 350°F and line a half sheet pan with aluminum foil, but do not grease. Set aside.

Begin by whisking the melted butter or oil in a large bowl along with both sugars, applesauce, and vanilla extract. Stir until fully incorporated and the mixture is homogenous.

In a separate bowl, sift the flour, cocoa, salt, baking powder, and baking soda. Whisk briefly to combine. Add the chocolate chips and toss to coat.

Pour the liquid ingredients into the bowl of dry and use a wide spatula to fold the two together. Stir until just combined. Transfer to your prepared sheet pan and smooth out into one even layer. Bake for 20 to 24 minutes, until it appears dry across the top and is pulling away from the sides slightly.

Cool completely before placing in the fridge to chill.

To prepare the ice cream filling, without shaking the cans of coconut milk, carefully open them and skim the thick cream off the top. Save the thin liquid at the bottom for another recipe (such as a smoothie or curry).

Use a stand mixer with a whisk attachment, a hand mixer, or just a good old-fashioned whisk to begin whipping the cream.

Sift in the confectioners' sugar and cocoa, a little bit at a time, while continuing to whisk. Add the vanilla last and whip until light and fluffy; 5 to 8 minutes.

(Continued on page 210)

To assemble, retrieve the cookie bar sheet and cut it in half crosswise, making sure the resulting two rectangles are the same size. Return one half to the pan but flip it with the top facing down. This gives you a flat platform to spread the whipped chocolate coconut cream on top. Smooth it out all the way to the sides and place the second half of the cookie sheet on top, with the right side facing up. Press down gently to adhere.

Set the jumbo ice cream sandwich on a flat surface in your freezer and let rest until solidified; at least 4 hours, and ideally overnight.

To serve, slice into individual rectangles and enjoy right away. To save the sandwiches for later, wrap each one in plastic and stash in an airtight container in the freezer for up to 6 months.

INDOOR S'MORES

MAKES 24 TO 30 SERVINGS

Get the full campfire experience without the mosquitos, sunburn, or lack of Wi-Fi! There's no need for roughing it with this full sheet of s'more satisfaction. Starting with a thick graham cracker crust, a super gooey chocolate filling melts in your mouth, crowned by a toasted marshmallow topping. It's every bit as sweet when you take this party inside!

GRAHAM CRACKER CRUST:

1 (14.4-ounce) box graham crackers, crushed (27 full rectangular sheets)
1 tablespoon ground flaxseeds
¼ teaspoon ground cinnamon
¼ teaspoon salt
¼ cup coconut oil or vegan butter, melted
⅔ cup water

GOOEY GANACHE FILLING:

1 cup granulated sugar
¾ cup Dutch-process cocoa powder
¼ teaspoon salt
½ cup vegan butter
¼ cup plain non-dairy milk

TOASTED MARSHMALLOW TOPPING:

½ cup aquafaba
1 cup granulated sugar
¼ teaspoon cream of tartar
1 teaspoon vanilla extract

Preheat your oven to 350°F and lightly grease a half sheet pan.

Place the graham crackers in your food processor and pulse to grind them down to fine crumbs. Remove large pieces and return them to the food processor if needed, to keep the texture consistent. Transfer to a large bowl and toss in the flaxseeds, cinnamon, and salt. Drizzle evenly with the melted oil or vegan butter and water, stirring thoroughly to combine.

Press the crust mixture into the bottom of your prepared pan, smoothing it firmly into an even layer. You may want to use the bottom of a lightly greased measuring cup or flat drinking glass for a perfectly flat surface.

Bake for 10 to 12 minutes, until no longer shiny, and set like a large cookie.

Meanwhile, prepare the chocolate filling by mixing the sugar, cocoa, and salt together in a small bowl. Add the melted vegan butter and non-dairy milk. Whisk vigorously to incorporate and continue stirring until the sugar has dissolved. It helps to start with very hot melted butter and non-dairy milk, so you may need to reheat them briefly in the microwave if the mixture still feels granular after a few minutes.

Spread the gooey chocolate all over the graham cracker crust, smoothing it into an even layer. Place the whole sheet pan in the fridge and let chill for at least 30 minutes before proceeding.

Finally for the meringue topping, preheat broiler to high.

(Continued on page 213)

Pour the aquafaba into the bowl of your stand mixer with the whisk attachment installed and gradually increase the speed up to its highest setting. Once you have a steady froth going, slowly sprinkle in the sugar and cream of tartar together. Whip at full power for 5 to 7 minutes, until you achieve a sturdy meringue that stands up at firm peaks.

Spread meringue over the cooled chocolate and graham crust. Broil for 2 to 4 minutes, or until the meringue topping is toasted and golden-brown. Let stand 5 minutes and cut into squares. Serve warm or at room temperature.

JUMBO CRUMB APPLE CRUMBLE

MAKES 10 TO 12 SERVINGS

For crust-lovers that are more about the pastry than the pie, I've got you. Let's flip this one upside-down, piling thick layers of buttery streusel that would be enough to make the average cobbler buckle. This hybrid crisp-meets-cake cuts out the middleman to get straight to the good stuff. Supple, fork-tender fruit melts beneath a blanket of brown sugar morsels infused with a touch of warm cinnamon spice.

CRUMB TOPPING:

1 cup vegan butter, melted
1⅓ cups coconut sugar or dark brown
    sugar, firmly packed
1½ teaspoons ground cinnamon
½ teaspoon salt
1¾ cups all-purpose flour

APPLE FILLING:

4 pounds (10–11 medium) sweet
    red apples, such as gala, fuji, or
    honeycrisp
¼ cup orange juice
1 teaspoon orange zest
¼ cup coconut sugar or dark brown
    sugar, firmly packed
1½ teaspoons ground cinnamon
½ teaspoon ground ginger
¼ teaspoon ground cloves
¼ teaspoon ground cardamom,
    optional
¼ teaspoon salt

Preheat your oven to 350°F and line a half sheet pan with aluminum foil. Spray the foil with nonstick cooking spray.

Prepare the crumb topping first, so it has time to set before baking. In a large bowl, combine the melted butter, sugar, cinnamon, and salt. Once thoroughly combined and homogeneous, introduce the flour. Stir vigorously to incorporate, switching over to a sturdy spoon or even your hands if needed. The resulting dough will be very thick and stiff, like you would expect to see for snickerdoodle cookies. Let rest in the fridge while you turn your attention to the fruit.

Peel, core, and roughly chop the apples, placing the pieces in a large bowl. Toss with the orange juice as you work to prevent them from browning. Add the zest, sugar, cinnamon, ginger, cloves, cardamom (if using), and salt. Mix thoroughly, taking care to evenly coat all the apples with the spices.

Transfer the fruit mixture to your prepared sheet pan, spreading it out to evenly fill the space. Retrieve the crumb topping from the fridge and use your fingers to crumble it into chunks about the size of raisins. No need to be too meticulous though; it's good to have some variation here for more texture. Sprinkle the crumbs all over the layer of apples as evenly as possible.

Bake for 40 to 45 minutes, until the apples are tender, and the crumb topping is golden-brown. Let cool for at least 10 minutes before digging in. The crumble is best served warm, with a scoop of ice cream slowly melting on top, ideally, but just as delightful at room temperature.

NEW YORK CRUMB CAKE

MAKES 15 TO 18 SERVINGS

Everyone knows that the best part of a crumb cake is the crumb topping, so let's not waste time with a thick layer of cake and get right to the good stuff. Styled after the monstrous streusel-encrusted slabs found in New York bakeries, the shallow walls of a standard sheet pan ensure that the crumb gets top billing in this classic dessert. It may even seem like too much of a good thing as it piles up high in the pan, but once you stick a fork in it, any doubts will be erased. This is the ideal ratio you've been craving all along.

CINNAMON CRUMB TOPPING:

2 cups dark brown sugar, firmly
    packed
1 tablespoon ground cinnamon
½ teaspoon salt
1 cup vegan butter, at room
    temperature
2 cups all-purpose flour

VANILLA CAKE:

3 cups all-purpose flour
1 cup granulated sugar
2 teaspoons baking powder
1 teaspoon baking soda
½ teaspoon salt
1½ cups unsweetened applesauce
½ cup olive oil
½ cup plain non-dairy milk
1 tablespoon apple cider vinegar
1 tablespoon vanilla extract

Preheat your oven to 350°F and line a quarter sheet pan with aluminum foil. Lightly grease and set aside.

Prepare the crumb topping first by placing the brown sugar, cinnamon, and salt in a medium bowl. Add the butter and use a potato masher to cream it in. Once fairly smooth, add the flour and mix with a fork to incorporate. Mix vigorously to incorporate the flour, forming small to medium clumps. You may need to use your hands if it seems a bit dry, but do not add water and do not overmix, or it will turn into a paste. Stash the crumb mixture in the fridge to chill while you prepare the cake.

Whisk together the flour, sugar, baking powder, baking soda, and salt in a large bowl. In a separate bowl, combine the applesauce, oil, non-dairy milk, vinegar, and vanilla, stirring until smooth. Pour the liquid ingredients into the bowl of dry and use a wide spatula to fold the two components together. The resulting batter should be rather thick.

Pour the batter into your prepared sheet pan, smoothing out the top with your spatula. Tap the pan a few times on the counter to release any air bubbles. Retrieve the crumb topping from the fridge, breaking it up a bit with a fork if it seems to have fused together. Sprinkle it evenly and generously all over the surface of the cake.

Bake in the center of your oven for 30 to 35 minutes, until golden-brown all over and a toothpick inserted into the center comes out clean. Let cool completely in the pan before slicing and serving.

PEACHES AND CREAM COBBLER

MAKES 12 TO 16 SERVINGS

Swept up in peach madness every summer, those impeccably juicy pink or orange orbs are impossible to resist. No matter how many I have already chilling in the fridge, I can't fight the urge to grab just a few more. Their season is so fleeting, it couldn't hurt to grab just another pound or two, right?

Thus, when you're overloaded with stone fruit that's ripe to bursting, a cream-filled cobbler will make quick work of any excess. Tender cornmeal biscuits bake right on top for a golden bite that sings of nostalgia for lazy days and star-filled nights. After the sun has set and the heat of the day subsides, pop this homey dessert into the oven to enjoy it right away, still warm, and ideally with a scoop of ice cream melting into every custard-filled crevasse.

PEACHES AND CREAM:

3 pounds (about 10–12) fresh peaches, pitted and sliced
½ cup granulated sugar, divided
2 tablespoons tapioca starch, divided
1 (8-ounce) package vegan cream cheese
¼ cup aquafaba
1 teaspoon vanilla extract

CORNMEAL BISCUIT TOPPING:

1 cup white whole wheat or all-purpose flour
1 cup coarse yellow cornmeal
¼ cup granulated sugar
2 teaspoons baking powder
½ teaspoon salt
⅛ teaspoon ground black pepper
½ cup coconut milk
⅓ cup olive oil

Preheat your oven to 350°F and lightly grease a half sheet pan.

Prepare the peaches first by tossing them in a large bowl with 2 tablespoons of the sugar and 1 tablespoon of the tapioca starch. Once evenly coated, transfer them to your sheet pan and spread them out evenly, without overlapping. It may seem like a sparse layer right now but fear not: The cream component will go a long way to fill the gaps.

Rinse out the bowl and add the remaining sugar and starch, along with the cream cheese. Beat vigorously with a spatula to combine. Add in the aquafaba and vanilla, whisking until completely smooth.

Spoon dollops of the cream all over the sheet pan at random, on top of and around the peach slices, until the mixture is used up.

For the topping, combine the flour, cornmeal, sugar, baking powder, salt, and pepper in a large bowl. Stir in the coconut milk and olive oil, switching out the spatula and using your hands to mix if the dough becomes too stiff to effectively manage.

Use a small cookie scoop (1½–2 tablespoons) to scoop out mini drop biscuits on top of the peaches and cream. Distribute them randomly, but fairly evenly, to make sure everyone gets one or two biscuits in every serving.

Bake for 30 to 32 minutes, until the cornmeal biscuits are golden-brown, and the cream has set. Let cool for at least 10 minutes before serving. Enjoy warm or at room temperature.

PEANUT BUTTERSCOTCH BLONDIES

MAKES 24 TO 30 BLONDIES

Infusing classic butterscotch blondies with an extra dollop of peanut buttery goodness elevates this humble bar cookie to all new heights. Spiked with coarse salt to amplify those nutty flavors further, each chewy bite crackles with crisp peanuts for the ideal balance between sweet and savory, soft and crunchy. Forget about the average peanut butter cookie; this generous tray of peanut butter perfection is even easier to whip up for feeding a crowd and has a greater range of textural options. Whether you go for the edge pieces or the gooey middle, you won't be disappointed.

3½ cups dark brown sugar, firmly packed
1 cup coconut oil or vegan butter, melted
1 cup crunchy peanut butter
½ cup unsweetened applesauce
½ cup aquafaba
1 tablespoon scotch, whisky, or bourbon
1 teaspoon vanilla extract
1 teaspoon salt
3⅔ cups all-purpose flour
1 teaspoon baking soda
½ teaspoon baking powder
2 cups whole, unsalted, roasted peanuts
½ teaspoon flaky or coarse salt (optional)

Preheat your oven to 350°F and line a half sheet pan with parchment paper or aluminum foil. Lightly grease and set aside.

Place the brown sugar in a large bowl and pour in the melted oil or butter. Stir vigorously until all the granules of sugar have dissolved. Add in the peanut butter, applesauce, and aquafaba, beating thoroughly with a wide spatula to combine. Add the scotch, vanilla, and salt, mixing well.

Sift the flour into the bowl along with the baking soda and powder. Add the peanuts, tossing to coat, and stir the whole mixture together to create a thick batter.

Spread the batter evenly into your prepared sheet pan, smoothing out the top with your spatula. Sprinkle evenly with flaky or coarse salt, if desired. Carefully move it into the middle of your oven and bake for 28 to 30 minutes, until golden-brown around the edges, crackled across the top, but still soft in the center.

Let cool at least 30 minutes before cutting; for best results, thoroughly chill in the fridge.

STRAWBERRY-RHUBARBARIAN BARS

MAKES 16 TO 24 SERVINGS

Technically a recipe testing failure, what was intended as a slab pie took on a life of its own. With a crust too soft to call a proper pastry and filling made from fruit that was too juicy, they're downright barbaric, terribly uncivilized compared to a classic composed dessert. Barbarians aren't known for their etiquette, but they do know how to have a good time. It's impossible to deny the fresh, sweet-tart-tangy flavor of such delightfully messy morsels. Manners be damned, dig in and don't worry about making it "perfect!"

PASTRY BASE:

1¾ cups oat flour

1 cup blanched almond flour

¼ cup melted vegan butter or coconut oil

¼ cup maple syrup

¼ teaspoon salt

STRAWBERRY FILLING:

1½ cups granulated sugar

⅓ cup cornstarch

1½ tablespoons agar powder

½ teaspoon salt

2½ cups lemon-lime soda

2 tablespoons beet juice (optional, for color)

2 pounds fresh strawberries, hulled and sliced

¼ pound fresh rhubarb, diced

Preheat your oven to 325°F and lightly grease a half sheet pan.

Beginning with the pastry, mix together both flours, melted butter or coconut oil, maple syrup, and salt until thoroughly combined. Transfer to your prepared sheet pan and use lightly moistened hands to press it down in an even layer. Use a fork to prick the surface evenly, to prevent any air bubbles from being trapped underneath.

Bake for 10 to 15 minutes or until light brown all over. Remove from oven and cool.

Meanwhile, combine the sugar, cornstarch, agar, and salt in a medium saucepan. Whisk to combine before slowly pouring in the soda, allowing the bubbles to subside before proceeding. Stir gently while adding the beet juice, if using, whisking until incorporated. Set over medium heat and bring to a boil. The sugar should be completely dissolved.

Scatter the sliced strawberries and rhubarb evenly over the baked pastry. Pour the hot liquid mixture on top, being careful not to disturb the fruit, covering all the pieces from corner to corner.

Return the sheet to the oven and bake for 20 to 25 minutes longer, until bubbling around the edges.

Let cool completely before placing in the fridge to fully set; about 2 hours. Slice and serve with ice cream or whipped coconut cream, if desired.

THAI TEA SHEET CAKE

MAKES 12 TO 16 SERVINGS

Perhaps it's unfair to appraise an eatery based on their drinks, but for me, Thai restaurants live or die by their Thai tea. Watching thick condensed milk swirl into vibrant rust-colored Assam tea is downright hypnotizing, pulling you in before the very first sip. Heady sweetness gives way to subtly spicy notes, enigmatic, mysterious, and entirely compelling. Ready-made mixes exist for those who want the authentic flavor without any of the extra work, but there's no way around those pesky artificial ingredients.

Start from scratch to unlock a bold new world of Thai tea possibilities, starting with dessert first! Steeped tea is baked right into this rich crumb, which is given somewhat of a tres leches treatment with condensed coconut milk. Soaking in every drop of syrup, it's finished with a fluffy topping of whipped coconut cream. It might not quench your thirst for an iced latte, but it will definitely satisfy your cravings.

SPONGE CAKE:

2 cups water
¼ cup black Assam or Ceylon tea leaves
4 whole star anise
1 tablespoon apple cider vinegar
3 cups all-purpose flour
1⅓ cups granulated sugar
2 teaspoons baking powder
1 teaspoon baking soda
½ teaspoon ground cardamom
¼ teaspoon ground cloves
½ teaspoon salt
1 cup olive oil
1 tablespoon vanilla extract

CONDENSED COCONUT MILK SYRUP:

1 (14-ounce) can full-fat coconut milk
1 cup confectioners' sugar

WHIPPED COCONUT CREAM:

1 (14-ounce) can full-fat coconut milk, chilled

Preheat your oven to 350°F and lightly grease a quarter sheet pan or 9 × 13-inch baking dish.

To make the cake, first prepare the Thai tea. In a small saucepan over medium heat, combine the water with the tea leaves and star anise. Bring just to the brink of a boil, cover, and remove from the stove. Let steep for 30 minutes. Strain out and discard the spent tea leaves and spices. Add the vinegar to the liquid tea.

In a separate bowl, combine the flour, sugar, baking powder and soda, cardamom, cloves, and salt. Add in the brewed and cooled tea mixture followed by the oil and vanilla. Stir just to combine, being careful not to over-mix.

Transfer the batter to your prepared pan, smoothing it across the bottom with your spatula. Bake for 28 to 34 minutes, until golden-brown all over and a toothpick inserted into the center comes out clean.

Quickly whisk together the coconut milk and confectioners' sugar to create the syrup. Pour it all over the cake while it's still hot. It may seem like a lot of liquid, but don't worry! It will absorb over time. Let cool completely before stashing in the fridge to chill; at least 2 to 3 hours.

To prepare the whipped coconut, without shaking the can, skim the thick cream off the top, saving the thin liquid at the bottom for another recipe (such as a smoothie or curry). Use a stand mixer with a whisk attachment, a hand mixer, or just a good old-fashioned whisk to whip the cream until thick and fluffy. Spread all over the top of the cake right before serving and enjoy cold.

WHOLE COCONUT HAUPIA

MAKES 32 SQUARES

Cool and refreshing like a tropical breeze, Haupia is a sweet staple of all Hawaiian luaus. Softly set to the consistency of flan, it trembles with a gentle touch, melting away easily into pure coconut bliss. Modern renditions frequently use coconut milk and gelatin, but there's a better way to get even fresher flavor: Go straight to the source with whole coconuts! Young coconuts, otherwise known as green coconuts, have tender, fragrant, almost jelly-like meat and lots of water within. Brown, mature coconuts, on the other hand, have a thick, hairy husk and are much harder and dryer. Shop carefully for the best ingredients; with so few, they all really count!

2 young coconuts
1 cup granulated sugar
1 cup cornstarch or potato starch

Preheat your oven to 350°F. Lightly grease a quarter sheet pan and set aside.

Carefully open the coconuts, reserving the water inside. Use a sturdy spoon to scoop out the meat and place it in your blender, along with the water. Thoroughly puree on the highest setting, until the mixture is completely smooth. Add regular water so that the total volume of liquid reaches 3 cups, along with the sugar and starch, blending once more to incorporate. Pause to scrape down the sides of the canister if needed, to ensure there are no clumps remaining that the blades have missed.

Transfer the coconut mixture to your prepared sheet pan and cover with aluminum foil. Very carefully place it on the center rack in your oven. Bake for 1 hour or until knife inserted in the middle comes out clean.

Let the haupia cool at room temperature before transferring it to the fridge to chill. Allow at least 2 hours before slicing into approximately 1-inch cubes and serving. Cover with plastic wrap and store in the fridge for up to 3 days.

Index

A

adobo
  Southwestern Wedge Salad, 80
All-Kale Caesar, 63
almonds
  Apricot-Almond Clafoutis, 199
  Charred Broccoli Crunch Salad, 68
  Nuthouse Stuffing, 100
  Oatsome Energy Bars, 49
Aloha Ramen Slaw, 64
Apple-Cinnamon Peanut Butter Bostock, 3
apple juice concentrate
  Apple-Cinnamon Peanut Butter Bostock, 3
apples
  Apple-Cinnamon Peanut Butter Bostock, 3
  Charred Broccoli Crunch Salad, 68
  Harvest Tagine, 161–162
  Jumbo Crumb Apple Crumble, 214
  Nuthouse Stuffing, 100
applesauce
  Cherry-Cola Texas Sheet Cake, 205–207
  Double Dark Fudgewiches, 208–210
  Jalapeño Cornbread, 94
  New York Crumb Cake, 217
  Oatmeal Cookie Baked Oatmeal, 16
  Oatsome Energy Bars, 49
  Peanut Butterscotch Blondies, 221
Apricot-Almond Clafoutis, 199
aquafaba
  Brownie Crisps, 200
  Carrot Cake Roulade, 203–204
  Pretzel Focaccia, 53
artichoke hearts
  Blistered Green Bean Niçoise Salad, 67
  Greek Three-Bean Salad, 75

  Paella Huerta, 176
arugula
  Hungry, Hungry Hippie Panini, 164
asparagus
  Minestrone Primavera, 126
  Tempeh Piccata, 193
avocado
  Aloha Ramen Slaw, 64
  Black Bean Chilaquiles, 7
  Furikake Avocado Fries, 38
  Hungry, Hungry Hippie Panini, 164
  Nacho Mamma Loaded Tortilla Chips, 46
  Southwestern Wedge Salad, 80

B

Baby Corn Esquites, 89
Banana Sheet Pan Cakes, 4
barley
  Mushroom Barley Soup, 129
BBQ Baked Bean Loaded Potatoes, 143–144
beans
  black
    Black Bean Chilaquiles, 7
    Championship Four-Pepper Chili, 118
    Nacho Mamma Loaded Tortilla Chips, 46
    Spicy Sichuan Snow Peas, 111
  chickpeas
    Chickpea Pan Pie, 149
    Chickpea Tikka Masala, 150
    Curried Naan Panzanella, 72
    Dill Pickle Chickpea Crunchies, 32
    Greek Three-Bean Salad, 75
    Hot Smashed Hummus, 42
  Garlicky Greens and Beans Stew, 125

green
  Blistered Green Bean Niçoise Salad, 67
  Greek Three-Bean Salad, 75
  Paella Huerta, 176
  Tempeh Piccata, 193
lentils
  Pumpkin Khichdi, 130
  Spaghetti Squash Bolognese, 189
pinto
  BBQ Baked Bean Loaded Potatoes, 143–144
  Chipotle Pozole, 121
red kidney
  Sheet Loaf with Mashed Cauliflower, 180–182
Roasted Zucchini and Chickpeas en Brodo, 134
white
  BBQ Baked Bean Loaded Potatoes, 143–144
  Chakalaka, 146
  Greens and Beans Crostini, 41
  Super Corny Quesadilla, 58
beet juice
  Strawberry-Rhubarbarian Bars, 222
  Super-Sized Pop Art Tart, 223–224
beets
  Minestrone Primavera, 126
  Ruby Beet Borscht, 137
  Spaghetti Squash Bolognese, 189
bell pepper
  Chakalaka, 146
  Championship Four-Pepper Chili, 118
  Chickpea Tikka Masala, 150
  Denver Omelet Roulade, 12
  Greek Three-Bean Salad, 75
  Hungry, Hungry Hippie Panini, 164
  Roasted Tomato Gazpacho, 133
  Southwestern Wedge Salad, 80
  Tofu Shakshuka, 26
Black Bean Chilaquiles, 7

Blistered Green Bean Niçoise Salad, 67
bourbon
  Peanut Butterscotch Blondies, 221
bread
  All-Kale Caesar, 63
  Apple-Cinnamon Peanut Butter Bostock, 3
  Greens and Beans Crostini, 41
  Hungry, Hungry Hippie Panini, 164
  Jalapeño Cornbread, 94
  Lavash Lasagna, 171
  naan
    Curried Naan Panzanella, 72
  Nuthouse Stuffing, 100
  Pretzel Focaccia, 53
  Pumpkin Parker House Rolls, 102–103
breadcrumbs
  Cauliflower Tempura, 31
  Sheet Loaf with Mashed Cauliflower, 180–182
broccoli
  Charred Broccoli Crunch Salad, 68
  General Tso's Tofu, 158
  Soy Curl Bulgogi with Broccoli, 186
broccoli rabe
  Greens and Beans Crostini, 41
Broiled Bhindi Masala, 90
Brownie Crisps, 200
Brussels sprouts
  Sweet Sesame Tofu and Roasted Brussels Sprouts, 190
  Warm Brussels Sprouts Salad, 84
bulgur
  Championship Four-Pepper Chili, 118
  Pesto Tabbouleh, 79

C
cabbage
  Aloha Ramen Slaw, 64
  Chipotle Pozole, 121
  Okonomiyaki, 50
  Ruby Beet Borscht, 137
  Sauerkraut Colcannon, 104

Steakhouse Cabbage with Horseradish
    Cream, 112
Yaki Udon Noodle Soup, 138
cakes
    Banana Sheet Pan Cakes, 4
    Cherry-Cola Texas Sheet Cake, 205–207
    New York Crumb Cake, 217
    Thai Tea Sheet Cake, 225
Canh Chua, 117
capers
    Blistered Green Bean Niçoise Salad, 67
    Harvest Tagine, 161–162
Carrot Cake Roulade, 203–204
carrots
    Chakalaka, 146
    Charred Broccoli Crunch Salad, 68
    Chickpea Pan Pie, 149
    Harvest Tagine, 161–162
    Minestrone Primavera, 126
    Miso-Ginger Glazed Carrots, 98
    Ruby Beet Borscht, 137
    Sunrise Scramble Sandwich, 20
    Tofu Fried Rice, 194
cashew butter
    Crispy Kale Salad, 71
cashews
    Crispy Kale Salad, 71
cauliflower
    Chickpea Tikka Masala, 150
    Dirty Riced Cauliflower, 154
    Sheet Loaf with Mashed Cauliflower,
        180–182
Cauliflower Tempura, 31
cereal
    Frosted Corn Flakes, 15
    Oatsome Energy Bars, 49
    rice
        Confetti Cake Granola, 11
Chakalaka, 146
Championship Four-Pepper Chili, 118

Charred Broccoli Crunch Salad, 68
cheese, vegan
    cream
        Carrot Cake Roulade, 203–204
        Denver Omelet Roulade, 12
        Hungry, Hungry Hippie Panini, 164
        Peaches and Cream Cobbler, 218
        Perfect Picnic Potato Salad, 76
    Parmesan
        Baby Corn Esquites, 89
cherries, maraschino
    Cherry-Cola Texas Sheet Cake, 205–207
Cherry-Cola Texas Sheet Cake, 205–207
chia seeds
    Oatsome Energy Bars, 49
    Puppy Training Treats, 54
Chickpea Pan Pie, 149
chickpeas
    Curried Naan Panzanella, 72
    Dill Pickle Chickpea Crunchies, 32
    Greek Three-Bean Salad, 75
    Hot Smashed Hummus, 42
    Roasted Zucchini and Chickpeas en Brodo,
        134
Chickpea Tikka Masala, 150
chilaquiles
    Black Bean Chilaquiles, 7
chili
    Championship Four-Pepper Chili, 118
chili sauce
    Cauliflower Tempura, 31
Chipotle Pozole, 121
chips
    Nacho Mamma Loaded Tortilla Chips, 46
    Sour Cream and Onion Zucchini Chips, 57
chocolate chips
    Banana Sheet Pan Cakes, 4
    Brownie Crisps, 200
    Confetti Cake Granola, 11
    Double Dark Fudgewiches, 208–210
cinnamon

Apple-Cinnamon Peanut Butter Bostock, 3
Cinnamon Sugar Sweet Potatoast, 8
cobbler
    Peaches and Cream Cobbler, 218
cocoa powder
    Championship Four-Pepper Chili, 118
    Cherry-Cola Texas Sheet Cake, 205–207
    Double Dark Fudgewiches, 208–210
    Indoor S'Mores, 211–213
coconut
    Aloha Ramen Slaw, 64
    Oatsome Energy Bars, 49
    Warm Brussels Sprouts Salad, 84
    Whole Coconut Haupia, 226
coffee, instant
    BBQ Baked Bean Loaded Potatoes,
        143–144
    Brownie Crisps, 200
    Championship Four-Pepper Chili, 118
cola
    Cherry-Cola Texas Sheet Cake, 205–207
Confetti Cake Granola, 11
corn
    Corn Pudding, 93
    Jalapeño Cornbread, 94
    Low Country Broil, 172
    Southwestern Wedge Salad, 80
    Super Corny Quesadilla, 58
cornbread
    Jalapeño Cornbread, 94
corn flakes
    Frosted Corn Flakes, 15
Corn Pudding, 93
couscous
    Harvest Tagine, 161–162
Crispy Kale Salad, 71
crumble
    Jumbo Crumb Apple Crumble, 214
cubanelle
    Championship Four-Pepper Chili, 118
cucumber

Chickpea Tikka Masala, 150
    Curried Naan Panzanella, 72
    Roasted Tomato Gazpacho, 133
Curried Naan Panzanella, 72

D

Dengaku Donburi, 153
Denver Omelet Roulade, 12
Dill Pickle Chickpea Crunchies, 32
Dirty Riced Cauliflower, 154
Double Dark Fudgewiches, 208–210

E

edamame
    Aloha Ramen Slaw, 64
eggplant
    Dengaku Donburi, 153
Eggplant Shawarma, 157
English muffins
    Sunrise Scramble Sandwich, 20

F

Falafel Panisse with Whipped Tahini, 35–36
fennel bulb
    Greek Three-Bean Salad, 75
flaxseeds
    Apple-Cinnamon Peanut Butter Bostock, 3
    Denver Omelet Roulade, 12
    Furikake Avocado Fries, 38
    Indoor S'Mores, 211–213
    Oatmeal Cookie Baked Oatmeal, 16
    Oatsome Energy Bars, 49
    Puppy Training Treats, 54
    Sheet Loaf with Mashed Cauliflower,
        180–182
French Onion Soup, 122
fries
    Furikake Avocado Fries, 38
Frosted Corn Flakes, 15
Furikake Avocado Fries, 38

G

Garlicky Greens and Beans Stew, 125
General Tso's Tofu, 158
gnocchi
    Kabocha Gnocchi with Miso Brewed Butter, 168
graham crackers
    Indoor S'Mores, 211–213
granola
    Confetti Cake Granola, 11
Greek Three-Bean Salad, 75
green chilies
    Denver Omelet Roulade, 12
Greens and Beans Crostini, 41
guacamole
    Black Bean Chilaquiles, 7

H

habanero
    Jerk Seitan with Tostones, 167
Harvest Tagine, 161–162
hash browns
    Spiralized Hash Browns, 19
haupia
    Whole Coconut Haupia, 226
hazelnuts
    Warm Brussels Sprouts Salad, 84
hemp seeds
    Furikake Avocado Fries, 38
hominy
    Chipotle Pozole, 121
horseradish
    Steakhouse Cabbage with Horseradish Cream, 112
hot sauce
    Baby Corn Esquites, 89
Hot Smashed Hummus, 42
hummus
    Hot Smashed Hummus, 42
    Hungry, Hungry Hippie Panini, 164
Hungry, Hungry Hippie Panini, 164

I

Indoor S'Mores, 211–213

J

Jalapeño Cornbread, 94
jalapeños
    Black Bean Chilaquiles, 7
    Chakalaka, 146
    Championship Four-Pepper Chili, 118
    Chickpea Tikka Masala, 150
    Dirty Riced Cauliflower, 154
    Nacho Mamma Loaded Tortilla Chips, 46
    Pumpkin Khichdi, 130
    Southwestern Wedge Salad, 80
    Super Corny Quesadilla, 58
Jerk Seitan with Tostones, 167
Jumbo Crumb Apple Crumble, 214

K

Kabocha Gnocchi with Miso Brewed Butter, 168
kale
    All-Kale Caesar, 63
    Crispy Kale Salad, 71
    Garlicky Greens and Beans Stew, 125

L

lasagna
    Lavash Lasagna, 171
Lavash Lasagna, 171
lentils
    Pumpkin Khichdi, 130
    Spaghetti Squash Bolognese, 189
lettuce
    Blistered Green Bean Niçoise Salad, 67
    Eggplant Shawarma, 157
    Mushroom Larb, 45
    Southwestern Wedge Salad, 80
Low Country Broil, 172

M

macadamia nuts
    Aloha Ramen Slaw, 64
Mad Mac & Peas, 175
maple syrup
    BBQ Baked Bean Loaded Potatoes,
        143–144
    Chakalaka, 146
    Charred Broccoli Crunch Salad, 68
    Confetti Cake Granola, 11
    Corn Pudding, 93
    Dengaku Donburi, 153
    Denver Omelet Roulade, 12
    Okonomiyaki, 50
    Strawberry-Rhubarbarian Bars, 222
    Sweet Sesame Tofu and Roasted Brussels
        Sprouts, 190
    Warm Brussels Sprouts Salad, 84
mayonnaise, vegan
    Baby Corn Esquites, 89
    Okonomiyaki, 50
Melting Za'atar Potatoes, 97
milk, non-dairy
    Apricot-Almond Clafoutis, 199
    Carrot Cake Roulade, 203–204
    coconut
        Chickpea Tikka Masala, 150
        Double Dark Fudgewiches, 208–210
        Thai Tea Sheet Cake, 225
    Mad Mac & Peas, 175
    Nacho Mamma Loaded Tortilla Chips, 46
    New York Crumb Cake, 217
    Oatmeal Cookie Baked Oatmeal, 16
    Sheet Loaf with Mashed Cauliflower,
        180–182
Minestrone Primavera, 126
mint
    Mushroom Larb, 45
miso
    All-Kale Caesar, 63
    Blistered Green Bean Niçoise Salad, 67

Dengaku Donburi, 153
    Kabocha Gnocchi with Miso Brewed Butter,
        168
    Lavash Lasagna, 171
    Perfect Picnic Potato Salad, 76
Miso-Ginger Glazed Carrots, 98
molasses, pomegranate
    Soy Curl Bulgogi with Broccoli, 186
Mushroom Barley Soup, 129
Mushroom Larb, 45
mushrooms
    Championship Four-Pepper Chili, 118
    Garlicky Greens and Beans Stew, 125
    Mushroom Barley Soup, 129
    Paella Huerta, 176
    Portobello Paprikash, 179
    Sheet Pan Pizza, 183–185
    Yaki Udon Noodle Soup, 138
mustard
    All-Kale Caesar, 63
    Blistered Green Bean Niçoise Salad, 67
    Charred Broccoli Crunch Salad, 68
    Denver Omelet Roulade, 12
    Mad Mac & Peas, 175
    Perfect Picnic Potato Salad, 76

N

Nacho Mamma Loaded Tortilla Chips, 46
New York Crumb Cake, 217
noodles
    Aloha Ramen Slaw, 64
    Yaki Udon Noodle Soup, 138
nori
    Furikake Avocado Fries, 38
    Okonomiyaki, 50
Nuthouse Stuffing, 100

O

Oatmeal Cookie Baked Oatmeal, 16
oats
    Confetti Cake Granola, 11

Oatmeal Cookie Baked Oatmeal, 16
Oatsome Energy Bars, 49
Puppy Training Treats, 54
Oatsome Energy Bars, 49
Okonomiyaki, 50
okra
Broiled Bhindi Masala, 90
olives
Blistered Green Bean Niçoise Salad, 67
Greek Three-Bean Salad, 75
onion
French Onion Soup, 122
orange juice
Aloha Ramen Slaw, 64
Jerk Seitan with Tostones, 167

P

Paella Huerta, 176
pasta
Mad Mac & Peas, 175
Minestrone Primavera, 126
Portobello Paprikash, 179
pastry, puff
Chickpea Pan Pie, 149
Peaches and Cream Cobbler, 218
peanut butter
Apple-Cinnamon Peanut Butter Bostock, 3
Peanut Butterscotch Blondies, 221
Puppy Training Treats, 54
Peanut Butterscotch Blondies, 221
peanuts
Apple-Cinnamon Peanut Butter Bostock, 3
Mushroom Larb, 45
Nuthouse Stuffing, 100
peas
Chickpea Pan Pie, 149
Mad Mac & Peas, 175
Minestrone Primavera, 126
Paella Huerta, 176
snow
Spicy Sichuan Snow Peas, 111

sugar snap
Snappy Snap Pea Risotto, 108
Tofu Fried Rice, 194
pecans
Carrot Cake Roulade, 203–204
Cinnamon Sugar Sweet Potatoast, 8
Kabocha Gnocchi with Miso Brewed Butter, 168
Nuthouse Stuffing, 100
pepitas
Black Bean Chilaquiles, 7
Perfect Picnic Potato Salad, 76
Pesto Tabbouleh, 79
pineapple
Canh Chua, 117
pineapple juice
Denver Omelet Roulade, 12
pine nuts
Harvest Tagine, 161–162
Pesto Tabbouleh, 79
pizza
Sheet Pan Pizza, 183–185
plantain
Jerk Seitan with Tostones, 167
poblano
Championship Four-Pepper Chili, 118
pop tart
Super-Sized Pop Art Tart, 23–24
Portobello Paprikash, 179
potatoes
BBQ Baked Bean Loaded Potatoes, 143–144
Blistered Green Bean Niçoise Salad, 67
Low Country Broil, 172
Melting Za'atar Potatoes, 97
Perfect Picnic Potato Salad, 76
russet
Spiralized Hash Browns, 19
Sauerkraut Colcannon, 104
sweet
Cinnamon Sugar Sweet Potatoast, 8

Garlicky Greens and Beans Stew, 125
Tempeh Piccata, 193
preserves
Super-Sized Pop Art Tart, 23–24
Pretzel Focaccia, 53
Pumpkin Khichdi, 130
Pumpkin Parker House Rolls, 102–103
pumpkin puree
Mad Mac & Peas, 175
Puppy Training Treats, 54
Puppy Training Treats, 54

Q

quesadilla
Super Corny Quesadilla, 58

R

radish
Chipotle Pozole, 121
Minestrone Primavera, 126
raisins
Harvest Tagine, 161–162
Oatsome Energy Bars, 49
rhubarb
Strawberry-Rhubarbarian Bars, 222
rice
arborio
Snappy Snap Pea Risotto, 108
brown
Sweet Sesame Tofu and Roasted
Brussels Sprouts, 190
Dengaku Donburi, 153
General Tso's Tofu, 158
Paella Huerta, 176
Portobello Paprikash, 179
Tofu Fried Rice, 194
risotto
Snappy Snap Pea Risotto, 108
Roasted Tomato Gazpacho, 133
Roasted Zucchini and Chickpeas en Brodo,
134

rolls
Pumpkin Parker House Rolls, 102–103
Ruby Beet Borscht, 137

S

salad
All-Kale Caesar, 63
Blistered Green Bean Niçoise Salad, 67
Charred Broccoli Crunch Salad, 68
Crispy Kale Salad, 71
Curried Naan Panzanella, 42
Greek Three-Bean Salad, 75
Perfect Picnic Potato Salad, 76
Southwestern Wedge Salad, 80
Tofu Caprese, 83
Warm Brussels Sprouts Salad, 84
sandwich
Sunrise Scramble Sandwich, 20
Sauerkraut Colcannon, 104
sausage, meatless
Low Country Broil, 172
Scalloped Summer Squash, 107
scotch
Peanut Butterscotch Blondies, 221
seitan
Jerk Seitan with Tostones, 167
Low Country Broil, 172
sesame seeds
Dengaku Donburi, 153
Furikake Avocado Fries, 38
Melting Za'atar Potatoes, 97
Soy Curl Bulgogi with Broccoli, 186
Sweet Sesame Tofu and Roasted Brussels
Sprouts, 190
shakshuka
Tofu Shakshuka, 26
Sheet Loaf with Mashed Cauliflower, 180–182
Sheet Pan Pizza, 183–185
Sichuan peppercorn
Spicy Sichuan Snow Peas, 111
Snappy Snap Pea Risotto, 108

soda
    Cherry-Cola Texas Sheet Cake, 205–207
soup
    Chipotle Pozole, 121
    French Onion Soup, 122
    Garlicky Greens and Beans Stew, 125
    Minestrone Primavera, 126
    Mushroom Barley Soup, 129
    Roasted Tomato Gazpacho, 133
    Roasted Zucchini and Chickpeas en Brodo, 134
    Ruby Beet Borscht, 137
    Yaki Udon Noodle Soup, 138
sour cream, vegan
    Steakhouse Cabbage with Horseradish Cream, 112
Sour Cream and Onion Zucchini Chips, 57
Southwestern Wedge Salad, 80
Soy Curl Bulgogi with Broccoli, 186
soy sauce
    Aloha Ramen Slaw, 64
    BBQ Baked Bean Loaded Potatoes, 143–144
    Canh Chua, 117
    Chickpea Pan Pie, 149
    Denver Omelet Roulade, 12
    French Onion Soup, 122
    General Tso's Tofu, 158
    Jerk Seitan with Tostones, 167
    Mushroom Barley Soup, 129
    Mushroom Larb, 45
    Okonomiyaki, 50
    Roasted Tomato Gazpacho, 133
    Sheet Loaf with Mashed Cauliflower, 180–182
    Soy Curl Bulgogi with Broccoli, 186
    Sweet Sesame Tofu and Roasted Brussels Sprouts, 190
    Tofu Fried Rice, 194
    Warm Brussels Sprouts Salad, 84
    Yaki Udon Noodle Soup, 138

Spaghetti Squash Bolognese, 189
Spicy Sichuan Snow Peas, 111
spinach
    Hungry, Hungry Hippie Panini, 164
    Minestrone Primavera, 126
Spiralized Hash Browns, 19
sprinkles
    Cherry-Cola Texas Sheet Cake, 205–207
    Confetti Cake Granola, 11
    Super-Sized Pop Art Tart, 23–24
squash
    Harvest Tagine, 161–162
    Kabocha Gnocchi with Miso Brewed Butter, 168
    Scalloped Summer Squash, 107
    Spaghetti Squash Bolognese, 189
sriracha
    Canh Chua, 117
    Cauliflower Tempura, 31
    General Tso's Tofu, 158
Steakhouse Cabbage with Horseradish Cream, 112
strawberries
    Banana Sheet Pan Cakes, 4
Strawberry-Rhubarbarian Bars, 222
stuffing
    Nuthouse Stuffing, 100
sunflower seeds
    Charred Broccoli Crunch Salad, 68
Sunrise Scramble Sandwich, 20
Super Corny Quesadilla, 58
Super-Sized Pop Art Tart, 23–24
sweet potatoes
    Cinnamon Sugar Sweet Potatoast, 8
    Garlicky Greens and Beans Stew, 125
Sweet Sesame Tofu and Roasted Brussels Sprouts, 190

T

tahini
    Falafel Panisse with Whipped Tahini, 35–36

Hot Smashed Hummus, 42
Nacho Mamma Loaded Tortilla Chips, 46
tea
    Thai Tea Sheet Cake, 225
tempeh
    BBQ Baked Bean Loaded Potatoes,
        143–144
    Dirty Riced Cauliflower, 154
    Low Country Broil, 172
    Mushroom Larb, 45
    Tempeh Piccata, 193
Tempeh Piccata, 193
Thai Tea Sheet Cake, 225
tofu
    Blistered Green Bean Niçoise Salad, 67
    Canh Chua, 117
    Dengaku Donburi, 153
    Denver Omelet Roulade, 12
    General Tso's Tofu, 158
    Lavash Lasagna, 171
    Perfect Picnic Potato Salad, 76
    Sunrise Scramble Sandwich, 20
    Sweet Sesame Tofu and Roasted Brussels
        Sprouts, 190
    Tofu Shakshuka, 26
    Yaki Udon Noodle Soup, 138
Tofu Caprese, 83
Tofu Fried Rice, 194
Tofu Shakshuka, 26
tomatoes
    Black Bean Chilaquiles, 7
    Broiled Bhindi Masala, 90
    Canh Chua, 117
    Chakalaka, 146
    Championship Four-Pepper Chili, 118
    cherry
        Blistered Green Bean Niçoise Salad, 67
        Broiled Bhindi Masala, 90
        Curried Naan Panzanella, 72
        Greek Three-Bean Salad, 75

Nacho Mamma Loaded Tortilla Chips,
    46
    Pesto Tabbouleh, 79
Chipotle Pozole, 121
Eggplant Shawarma, 157
Garlicky Greens and Beans Stew, 125
Pumpkin Khichdi, 130
Roasted Tomato Gazpacho, 133
Ruby Beet Borscht, 137
sundried
    Greens and Beans Crostini, 41
    Pesto Tabbouleh, 79
    Sheet Loaf with Mashed Cauliflower,
        180–182
Sunrise Scramble Sandwich, 20
Tofu Shakshuka, 26
tomato sauce
    General Tso's Tofu, 158
    Lavash Lasagna, 171
    Okonomiyaki, 50
    Sheet Loaf with Mashed Cauliflower,
        180–182
    Sheet Pan Pizza, 183–185
    Spaghetti Squash Bolognese, 189
tortillas
    Black Bean Chilaquiles, 7
    Southwestern Wedge Salad, 80
    Super Corny Quesadilla, 58

W
walnuts
    Brownie Crisps, 200
    Carrot Cake Roulade, 203–204
    Oatsome Energy Bars, 49
    Spaghetti Squash Bolognese, 189
Warm Brussels Sprouts Salad, 84
whisky
    Peanut Butterscotch Blondies, 221
Whole Coconut Haupia, 226

Y

Yaki Udon Noodle Soup, 138
yeast, nutritional
   All-Kale Caesar, 63
   Baby Corn Esquites, 89
   Crispy Kale Salad, 71
   Denver Omelet Roulade, 12
   Furikake Avocado Fries, 38
   Lavash Lasagna, 171
   Mad Mac & Peas, 175
   Nacho Mamma Loaded Tortilla Chips, 46
   Scalloped Summer Squash, 107
   Snappy Snap Pea Risotto, 108
   Sour Cream and Onion Zucchini Chips, 57
   Sunrise Scramble Sandwich, 20
   Super Corny Quesadilla, 58
   Tempeh Piccata, 193
   Tofu Shakshuka, 26

yogurt, vegan
   Cauliflower Tempura, 31
   Chickpea Tikka Masala, 150
   Corn Pudding, 93
   Eggplant Shawarma, 157
   Ruby Beet Borscht, 137
   Southwestern Wedge Salad, 80

Z

zucchini
   Harvest Tagine, 161–162
   Paella Huerta, 176
   Roasted Zucchini and Chickpeas en Brodo, 134
   Scalloped Summer Squash, 107
   Sour Cream and Onion Zucchini Chips, 57

Conversion Charts

METRIC AND IMPERIAL CONVERSIONS
(These conversions are rounded for convenience)

Ingredient	Cups/Tablespoons/Teaspoons	Ounces	Grams/Milliliters
Cornstarch	1 tablespoon	0.3 ounce	8 grams
Flour, all-purpose	1 cup/1 tablespoon	4.5 ounces/0.3 ounce	125 grams/8 grams
Flour, whole wheat	1 cup	4 ounces	120 grams
Fruit, dried	1 cup	4 ounces	120 grams
Fruits or veggies, chopped	1 cup	5 to 7 ounces	145 to 200 grams
Fruits or veggies, pureed	1 cup	8.5 ounces	245 grams
Liquids: milk, water, or juice	1 cup	8 fluid ounces	240 milliliters
Maple syrup or corn syrup	1 tablespoon	0.75 ounce	20 grams
Oats	1 cup	5.5 ounces	150 grams
Salt	1 teaspoon	0.2 ounce	6 grams
Spices: cinnamon, cloves, ginger, or nutmeg (ground)	1 teaspoon	0.2 ounce	5 milliliters
Sugar, brown, firmly packed	1 cup	7 ounces	200 grams
Sugar, white	1 cup/1 tablespoon	7 ounces/0.5 ounce	200 grams/12.5 grams
Vanilla extract	1 teaspoon	0.2 ounce	4 grams

OVEN TEMPERATURES

Fahrenheit	Celsius	Gas Mark
225°	110°	¼
250°	120°	½
275°	140°	1
300°	150°	2
325°	160°	3
350°	180°	4
375°	190°	5
400°	200°	6
425°	220°	7
450°	230°	8